A MAN OF FEW WORDS

The Westbourne Press
Gable House, 18–24 Turnham Green Terrace, London W4 1QP
www.westbournepress.co.uk

Published in Great Britain 2025 by The Westbourne Press

First published in Italian as *Un uomo di poche parole: Storia di Lorenzo, che salvò Primo* in 2023 by Editori Laterza, Roma-Bari

Copyright © 2023, Gius. Laterza & Figli
Translation © by Howard Curtis

Carlo Greppi has asserted his right under the Copyright, Designs and Patents Act, 1988, to be identified as the author of this work.

All rights reserved.

Every reasonable effort has been made to obtain the permissions for copyright material reproduced in this book. If any have been inadvertently overlooked, however, the publishers will correct this in future editions.

This book is sold subject to the condition that it shall not, by way of trade or otherwise, be lent, resold, hired out, or otherwise circulated without the publisher's prior consent in any form of binding or cover other than that in which it is published and without a similar condition including this condition being imposed on the subsequent purchaser.

ISBN 978 1 908906 61 8
eISBN 978 1 908906 62 5

The EU GPSR authorised representative is
Logos Europe, 9 rue Nicolas Poussin, 17000 La Rochelle, France.
E-mail: Contact@logoseurope.eu

Printed and bound by in Great Britain by Clays Ltd, Elcograf S.p.A.

This work has been translated with the contribution of the Centro per il libro e la lettura del Ministero della Cultura italiano.

Carlo Greppi

A MAN OF FEW WORDS

*The Bricklayer of Auschwitz
Who Saved Primo Levi*

TRANSLATED FROM ITALIAN BY
Howard Curtis

The Westbourne Press

CONTENTS

List of Illustrations — vii
Prologue — ix

PART I
1. Tacca From the Burgué — 3
2. Knives and Curses — 17
3. And Night Came — 28

PART II
4. Wasting Away — 45
5. The Language of Survival — 51
6. Working in 'Suiss' — 62

PART III
7. Messages — 73
8. The Night That Refuses to End — 96
9. Walking — 111

PART IV
10. Us Few Still Alive — 127
11. From One Who Always Remembers You — 154
12. And They Will Pay Back — 168
13. The Story of a Holy Drinker — 187
14. The Last Word — 196

Acknowledgements — 217
Notes — 224
Sources — 234
Credits — 236
Index — 238

ILLUSTRATIONS

Lorenzo Perrone, 1940s	6
Fossano, near the railway station, late 1800s	11
Fossano's old quarter (Borgo Vecchio), 1942	12
Lorenzo Perrone in the military, 1924	18
A note from Primo Levi on the way to Auschwitz, 1944	39
Soup ration distribution at Monowitz, early 1940s	53
Food stamps from Monowitz, 1944	74
A letter from Levi, sent by Perrone 1944	87
Another letter Levi, sent by Perrone 1944	105
Lorenzo Perrone's passport, 1942	120
Apprentice bricklayers in Fossano, early 1950s	156
Inhabitants of Fossano, 1943	157
Inhabitants of Fossano, 1947	157
Postcard from Lorenzo Perrone, 1946	158
Primo Levi with his son Renzo, 1959	197
The Perrone family home, 1980s	204

PROLOGUE

And I said to him: 'You're taking a big risk, talking to me.' And he said: 'I really don't care.'
— Primo Levi, November 1986

One December day several years ago, I found myself watching a documentary called *The Courage and the Pity*,[1] which describes the support – real and presumed – that persecuted Jews received from Italians during the Holocaust. Thanks to this support, though more than 7,000 of them perished, the majority of Italian Jews were saved.[2] The documentary was first broadcast in November 1986, five months before Primo Levi's death. Among the scenes that struck me was one in which Levi himself talked, with his usual composure, about a quiet man who had saved his life. This man was a humble bricklayer, a civilian worker from Fossano in Piedmont, who lived *outside* the barbed-wire fence surrounding Auschwitz III-Monowitz. Every day for six months, this man brought Levi soup, compensating for the malnutrition in the Lager. The only reward he accepted – if we can call it that – was to have his leather shoes repaired by the cobblers in the camp. During the four days it took to repair them, Perrone walked in Levi's wooden clogs.[3]

This wasn't the first time I had heard of Lorenzo Perrone. Levi first wrote about him in 1947 in his Holocaust memoir *If This Is A Man*, then in a handful of pages in *Moments of Reprieve*, as well as two passages in *The Drowned and The*

Saved – always omitting Lorenzo's surname. I already knew that both of Levi's children (Lisa Lorenza, born in 1948, and Renzo, born in 1957) owed their names to this mysterious man; I would later discover that Levi declared this publicly.[4] But hearing that Lorenzo risked ending up in Auschwitz himself because of his actions – and I mean hearing it *said*, not just reading it – moved something deep inside me. It touched a part of me that had long been asleep, or that had become hardened.

At about the same time, late one evening in December 2014, I put on a film before going to bed. I'd been planning to watch *The Judge of the Righteous*[5] for almost three years, but it had never made its way up the pile. In the very first scene, Mordecai Paldiel, then director of the Department of the Righteous Among the Nations, which recognises non-Jews who saved Jews at The World Holocaust Remembrance Center Yad Vashem in Jerusalem, picked up a file under the name of Lorenzo Perrone, file no. 8157. I went to the section of the Yad Vashem website devoted to the 25,271 'Righteous Among the Nations', 610 of whom were Italians.[6] I found an extract there from *If This Is A Man*:

> However little sense there may be in trying to specify why I, rather than thousands of others, managed to survive the test, I believe that it was really due to Lorenzo that I am alive today; and not so much for his material aid, as for his having constantly reminded me by his presence, by his natural and plain manner of being good, that there still existed a just world outside our own, something and someone still pure and whole, not corrupt, not savage, extraneous to hatred and terror; something difficult to

x

define, a remote possibility of good, but for which it was worth surviving.[7]

Primo Levi, perhaps the greatest witness of the twentieth century, wrote and said on many occasions – quite apart from those I've already cited – that he owed Lorenzo not only his life, but something more. Lorenzo Perrone is unique among the Righteous. His story should be better known at the level of Giorgio Perlasca and Oskar Schindler – made famous by Steven Spielberg's film *Schindler's List* (1993), based on a 1982 book by Thomas Keneally. Perrone is unusual in that he came from a completely different social context to other so-called saviours. This poor, troubled individual, 'almost illiterate'[8] and taciturn, 'was a man' – as Levi wrote – 'his humanity was pure and uncontaminated, he was outside this world of negation.' Levi shows his gratitude for Perrone with, 'thanks to Lorenzo, I managed not to forget that I myself was a man.'[9] It may well be that Perrone's simple, everyday acts were at the root of Levi's decision to bear witness to the Holocaust. The support Perrone gave is indelibly stamped on books that have formed a significant part of the culture of the Western world over the past half century.

But who was Lorenzo Perrone? In a posthumously published interview with *The Paris Review* in 1985, after declaring that Lorenzo was 'almost illiterate,' Levi added that they 'almost never spoke.' 'He was a silent man. He refused my thanks. He almost didn't reply to my words. He just shrugged: Take the bread, take the sugar. Keep silent, you don't need to speak.'

Over the years I have gathered material about Lorenzo's life before, during and after 'Suiss' (as he called Auschwitz).

He is present in the archives in Fossano, where we come across the first stumbling block: was his name Perrone or Perone? And in living memory – I have firsthand testimonies from two of his nephews. From the impracticable attempt to trawl through biographies and interviews by Primo Levi (more than 300 counted to date) and the thousands of books about Levi or his works (about 7,000 at the time of writing) for any mention of Lorenzo, to the file, now preserved in Yad Vashem, of the case undertaken in 1995 by biographer Carole Angier to elevate Lorenzo to a 'Righteous Among the Nations',[10] I have pieced together the life of Perrone. And that's just the beginning.

A considerable portion of what we can say about this remarkable man who made Levi's astonishing story of survival possible is there in Levi's texts. Having the work of one of the most accurate investigators of the human spirit to hand is the most extraordinary thing a historian can hope for. Levi's writing reveals the heart of humanity. But 'the reality of men is not the same as the reality of men as told by writers,' as Alberto Cavaglion, one of the subtlest connoisseurs of Levi's work, put it to me. This is something Primo Levi himself often spoke about: the art of 'rounding out,'[11] making use of the imagination, because 'reality is always more complex' and 'cruder.'[12]

It is hardly surprising that in such a humble life – such an *ordinary* life, until 'Suiss' – there are many gaps to be filled. Perrone's life was submerged before it emerges into the light. Still, the blanket of oblivion that fell over much of the existence of this man of few words can be pierced. This story begins with Levi and Perrone's first encounter, then retraces Perrone's steps that took him to Auschwitz – steps that had covered hundreds and hundreds of miles – before they reached the profound legacy left to us in this universal story of damnation and salvation.

This story transcends nationalities and borders and goes to the very essence of the human spirit, even though it was played out in very specific places and times: first Piedmont in Italy and France, then occupied Poland, then back again to Italy. Though the traces that have been left to us from those months in Auschwitz are few and far between, getting close to the details of what happened can help us to grasp their specificity and, at the same time, to illuminate their universality.

This is a story about the past, parts of which may become clearer than they really were, other parts more blurred. In sharing this search for meaning I'm hoping to clarify in my own mind why Lorenzo's story became an obsession – perhaps because of how it ends, perhaps because it might never have begun.

PART I

[...]
I speak for you, companions of a crowded
Road, not without its difficulties,
And for you too, who have lost
Soul, courage, the desire to live;
Or no one, or someone, or perhaps only one person,
   or you
Who are reading me: remember the time
Before the wax hardened,
When everyone was like a seal.
   Each of us bears the imprint
Of a friend met along the way;
In each the trace of each.
[...]

— Primo Levi, 'To My Friends'

CHAPTER I

Tacca From the *Burgué*

When he met Prisoner 174,517, Lorenzo was putting up a wall. Despite or perhaps because of the blows he had been dealt by life, even here he built his walls 'straight, solid, with well-staggered bricks and as much mortar as was required; not in deference to orders but out of professional dignity.'[1] These are Primo Levi's words, in *The Drowned and the Saved*.

When he saw the Turinese prisoner for the first time, Lorenzo, who was from the old quarter of Fossano, wasn't asking himself what and who would benefit from his backbreaking work. It was early summer of 1944, sometime between 16 and 21 June. An allied bombing raid had just damaged 'that immense tangle of iron, concrete, mud and smoke'[2] called 'the Buna', the great project of I. G. Farben in Monowitz, six kilometres from Auschwitz I. The whole site had been bent out of shape by Allied bombers, who struck the industrial plant, and later took aerial photographs of 'Planet Auschwitz', but did nothing to liberate the prisoners from the threat of the gas chamber. The western part of Upper Silesia was on a state of alert: in the months to come, it would be systematically subjected to increasingly spectacular bombing raids. After zigzagging between the rubble that crunched under the leather of his work shoes, Lorenzo and his fellow worker, another Italian, reached the

3

most valuable equipment. Their task was to protect it with high, sturdy walls and not complain too much about it.

Lorenzo was up on a scaffolding, laying bricks in silence. Prisoner 174,517, a nondescript *Häftling* with his number tattooed on his left arm, who Lorenzo would later discover was named Primo, was below him. Lorenzo told Primo in German that the cement had nearly run out and so he needed another bucket. The twenty-four-year-old, still only a number and worn down to almost nothing, spread his legs, seized the handle of the bucket with both hands, and tried to lift and swing it in such a way that he could take advantage of the momentum and move the load forward and, from there, onto his back. But the results proved pathetic to say the least and the bucket fell to the ground, spilling half the cement. Lorenzo hadn't found this funny.

'Well, what can you expect from people like this?'[3] Lorenzo had said as he prepared to descend. By the time he came down to the same level as the spilled cement, it was already hardening amid the rubble. Who was Lorenzo referring to when he said 'people like this'? Did he mean the 'slaves of the slaves',[4] 'the lowest rung' in the hierarchy of Monowitz? Or did he mean middle-class folk unable to keep hold of a bucket, people who'd been privileged until they entered this upside-down world, at which point they'd become the lowest of the low? The phrase oozes either contempt or commiseration – it's Levi himself who uses these words – and, at the same time, it shows a reversal of roles. Who knows how many times Lorenzo had heard it said of himself? He was a poor wretch, an alcoholic, prone to violence. Though he may also have been a good worker, you just can't trust 'people like this'. You take advantage of them until they reach the age of forty, when their strength starts to go and they lose concentration and then, when they're no more use, you get rid of them.

It was certainly not an auspicious first encounter between the two, considering what a mess Prisoner 174,517 had made. All the same, Primo Levi had been noticed by Lorenzo because of his curious reaction on hearing Italian, following the initial surly order given in bad German. Lorenzo's Italian, in a very recognisable Piedmontese accent, broke the spell that confined every human being to his or her place in the monumentally absurd universe of the Lager. Lorenzo had felt the overwhelming presence of this unqualified male workforce. Although inmates of other nationalities had the opportunity to establish contact with the outside world, for example, through the Frenchmen forced into the *Service du travail obligatoire*, as far as civilian workers like Lorenzo were concerned, the slaves were 'untouchables'. '[Civilians] think, more or less explicitly – with all the nuances lying between contempt and commiseration – that as we have been condemned to this life of ours, reduced to our condition, we must be tainted by some mysterious, grave sin,'[5] Primo Levi would recall.

Did Lorenzo think this, in that moment when he became aware of Levi? It seems unlikely, because he was not the kind of person to casually attribute blame. He knew that it's almost always the weak who are in chains, while the strong change their shoes every few weeks. Having gained something of an insight into his personality through a reasonable number of sources, I think that even in the two or three days that followed Lorenzo made no attempt to search for words: more likely, he mulled things over, with that inscrutable look on his face, partly lost, partly stern, the look we see in the photographs of him that have come down to us – as far as I know, there are only two. One of them we will see shortly; this is the other.

Lorenzo Perrone, 1940s.

Did Lorenzo feel contempt for this man who had almost vanished, this man at death's door? Did he feel pity? Was he afraid of him? Anxiety had risen with the introduction of the racial laws of 1938, which Primo Levi would describe in 1975 in *The Periodic Table*, recalling that first 'minuscule but perceptible flash of mistrust and suspicion. What do you think of me? What am I for you?'[6] I quote again from Levi, so good at weaving the words and concepts that help us understand the human spirit; here referring specifically to the way the civilian workers looked at the 'slaves of the slaves', the Jewish prisoners in their ragged striped uniforms and caps who were marched in a highly regimented manner to the Buna to work, if it could be described as work:

> They hear us speak in many different languages, which they do not understand and which sound to them as grotesque as animal noises. They see us reduced to ignoble slavery, without hair, without honour and without names, beaten every day, more abject every day, and they never see in our eyes a light of rebellion, or of peace, or of faith. They know us as thieves and untrustworthy, muddy, ragged and starving, and mistaking the effect for the cause, they judge us worthy of our abasement.[7]

How to capture the moment when this story started to become something more than a line in a buried archive? How to unite in a single snapshot the distance Lorenzo had travelled to work, head bowed, since he was a child? In vagabond lives, more than in any others, you must play your best hand. One image dominates: Lorenzo and Primo belonged 'to two different castes'[8] and might never have looked at each other. Not in their previous lives and not here, where privilege was reversed. Primo was destined to die, if he didn't use his wits each minute; Lorenzo to live, if he didn't get into trouble.

Lorenzo's superior position, both in spatial terms at that moment and in the hierarchy of the Lager, was a kind of retribution, considering their respective histories in the world as it was before, the world outside. Here, in 1944, privilege was in the ground Lorenzo walked on, he who had swallowed so much dust. In his previous life, Prisoner 174,517 had been a bourgeois with a decent income, the aspiring chemistry graduate Primo Levi. Now he was at the lowest point of the human spirit, a slave like I.G. Farben's 11,600 other workers. He did all kinds of exhausting jobs that year to build the Buna, the camp's chemical products factory. But his work, their work, was often 'pointless'[9] toil, intended to exhaust every fibre of their bodies until it killed them. In heavy rain or light snow, whether the wind blew away the ash or the sun threw it into sharp relief, Levi spent his day shovelling, burying, lifting, dropping, sorting and assembling until his veins and arteries were close to bursting. If he couldn't continue, he would be hit on the head with a shovel by a Kapo or someone else in charge. It was a reaffirmation of power and a destruction of what makes us human. But Primo didn't ask Lorenzo for help that day, I assume because at the time, with all that was happening in the summer of 1944, he didn't have 'a clear idea of how these Italians lived or what they could afford.'[10] In the world as it used to be, they were mostly poor wretches, but here they were on the surface, while he was sinking with thousands of other rejects into history itself. Yet all it took was a handful of words, barely tipping the scales of their common language, to break the spell: this is how 'the weapons of the night are blunted,'[11] as Levi would say.

Lorenzo was sparing with his words, it's true — but he did utter more after that initial awkward misunderstanding.

'You're taking a big risk, talking to me,' said Primo.

'I really don't care,' replied Lorenzo.[12]

...

A bricklayer, one who knows his job, builds.

Not that he has an overall vision — it's the person who gives orders, who tells him what to do, who has that — but he plays his part. I would hazard a guess that Lorenzo was one of the few who had that vision from the start, although I can't back that up: it's hard to find anyone who can claim they really knew him.

Lorenzo was a man of few words and he was always

on the move. In the 1930s, beginning in 1935 or 1936, he crossed over to France through the Finestre Pass to work illegally. He would cross the border clandestinely, with other poor wretches like him, his palms callused, his feet knobby and wrinkled from so much walking. His elder brother Giovanni, two years older than him, with his thin eyes and thick hair, would often be with him. They stepped out briskly side by side, along routes used by smugglers. They would sometimes walk continuously for a week to find work: that's the way things were. I can almost hear the smugglers with whom Lorenzo and Giovanni shared part of the way, speaking in Piemontese. '*Ndoma, 'mpresa*', 'come on, get on with it', the ritual admonition to anyone walking with head bowed, saving their energy for the work awaiting them. On those routes, where you might be a cross-border worker or a smuggler depending on the circumstances – the distinction between legal and illegal was very blurred – you met people of all ages coming in the opposite direction, from France to Italy. They spoke the same language, the language of the world's rejects, the wretched of the mountains, who sweat blood, in sun and rain, for a plate of stale polenta, and if they had to go to sleep without, would grin and bear it. Lorenzo's brother Giovanni, known as *barba Giuanin*, was definitely in France as early as August 1931. It was where their uncle, 'Jean', lived.

Giovanni would go to the Côte d'Azur, where 'there always was plenty of work,'[13] as Levi recalled, probably to Toulon or other towns in the south of France; more specifically to Embrun, a small town some sixty kilometres from the border. When the Giro d'Italia went through the Maddalena Pass, the old men would take advantage of the occasion to go up there by taxi and wave them on, and maybe have a drink or two. I'm told this in January 2020 by Lorenzo's nephew Beppe, son of another brother (Michele, eight years younger than Lorenzo). Beppe tells me that every trade had its patois, so you can't imagine them talking in Italian, they'd be using their own cryptic bricklayers' lingo.[14]

At lunchtime, Lorenzo would take out his aluminium mess tin, two eggs, a bottle of dark wine and some crusts of bread. He had an impressive body, but though he was between thirty-one and thirty-five at the time, his skin was leathery and it was already the body of an old man. The wooden spoon was like an extension of his arms, his trunk seemed anchored to the ground. He was from the *Burgué*, the old quarter of bricklayers and fishermen who earned some kind of living on the River Stura, eaten by mosquitoes as big as rats. It doesn't take much of an effort to visualise the *Burgué* as it was then, as the world plodded towards modernity. Photographs from the beginning of the twentieth century help too. All the doors open, worm-eaten chairs lined up against a tumbledown wall, absorbing the wind and the bitter cold, or good weather at weekends if the heavens granted it. Days that began in the dark and ended when there's still a little light, for those who manage to get home to sleep. It's all different now, but you can still glimpse traces of that old quarter as you make your way down the streets between newly repainted walls, even if the old names and house numbers have been changed.

Lorenzo lived about a kilometre from where the first photograph was taken, and a few metres from where the second was taken, specifically at nos. 4–6 Via Michelini, which today corresponds to No. 12. There were three rooms for eight people, one for rags and scrap metal, and

The *Burgué*, the old quarter of bricklayers and fishermen, in Fossano, Italy, late 1800s.

one for the mule and the cart.[15] At night the men raised eels by means of dykes and fished on the Stura with nets and lines; at dawn the women loaded this bounty and sold the fruit of their toil to people as poor as them. 'You did what you could, you sold what you made,'[16] you tried to keep out of trouble, apart from the occasional fight to test your own mortality, perhaps, or to forget your hunger. Ninety years later, with ill-concealed nostalgia, local people still remember that the men in the *Burgué* were all fishermen, or tinsmiths, or bricklayers like Lorenzo and Giovanni, and returned to the *Burgué* to sleep. The main streets were not paved until 1936. You never saw the sun between the houses, obscured as it was by the Umberto I barracks,[17] which no longer exist. As the two brothers walked along the street, looking down at the dust or the mud that's always there for those who have nothing, people would move aside, saying, 'Look, there are the giants.' This is what Beppe tells me.[18] 'Look, there are the *Tacca*.'[19]

...

Fossano's old quarter (Borgo Vecchio), 1942.

Lorenzo was the second child. His parents – Giuseppe and Giovanna Tallone, married in 1901 – lived off scrap iron and rags, although their official occupations were, respectively, 'bricklayer' and 'female worker'. Lorenzo had two other brothers who were tinsmiths – Beppe's father Michele and Secondo, who despite his name was actually the fourth and last male child. His two sisters were called Giovanna and Caterina. Caterina remained unmarried and later lived with Lorenzo and Giovanni, *barba Giuanin*.[20] Everyone in the fishermen's quarter of Fossano called the two brothers *Tacca*, short for *attaccabrighe*: troublemakers. None of the men in the family, including *Tacca el tule bel*, Michele 'the handsome tinsmith', spoke much, a trait they inherited from their father, who was 'withdrawn, and given to dark depressions.'[21] The expression in the portrait photograph that can still be seen on his grave is a severe one. Beneath scowling eyebrows, cold eyes and an unkempt moustache, it is hard to imagine a smile.

Giuseppe was 'harsh and tyrannical, often drunk, and when drunk, quarrelsome and violent.'[22] The childhood of Lorenzo, Giovanni and their siblings was punctuated by the many blows they received at home, and later, quite naturally, by those they themselves gave outside the 'Pigher' – the pub frequented by fishermen and bricklayers at the corner of Via Don Bosco and Via Garibaldi, not far from their home. The pub closed years ago, and the building in its place today doesn't look anything like it did then. It is painted clay red now. The four arches that once greeted Lorenzo and the rest of that clientele have been cleaned up. The street sign on the corner, *Terziere del Borgo Vecchio – Via Del Borgo Vecchio*, gleams, beautifying the image of that period. The passing of time can speak loudly; for others, it silences. The family of Luisa Mellano, president of the Fossano branch of the National Association of Partisans and great-niece of the legendary partisan Piero Cosa, lived opposite the 'Pigher', and her great-grandfather, a fisherman, drank there all the time, like dozens of others, she tells me. In winter the men, as was common then, wore short capes.[23] We can imagine them bent over their plates of liver through long evenings, men who worked their fingers to the bone went there to take a breather and eat a hot meal. Sometimes there were even priests among them. I imagine these men quoting verbatim a popular Fossano song from 1870, *I Monarca*: '*Soma busse 'n po' 'd barbera*': 'Let's go and drink a little Barbera.' General inebriation was guaranteed.

Part of the reason the Tacca were so silent was because of all the sharp, dark wine knocked back. Lorenzo and Giovanni, walking up and down the mountains, crossing borders, wearing out their shoes, really did drink. They'd probably been drinking since they were boys,[24] even though at the time it was forbidden by law to sell alcohol to those under the age of fourteen.

...

Lorenzo got by in many ways: the dominant idea was always, or almost always, to keep going. In early twentieth-century Italy, everything was bought and sold with a whisper and a handshake – 'you shook hands, and you had a deal.'[25] As a small boy following in his father's footsteps, Lorenzo took a stab at being a *feramiù*, a junk dealer: he would detach the lower piece of a drainpipe, which was of cast iron, and then lean out of the ground-floor window of his house and sell it to whoever passed by. Like Bartolomeo Vanzetti, the anarchist murdered in the United States in 1927, who was about twelve years older than Lorenzo and who had been born and raised ten kilometres from Fossano, and who at the age of fifteen was already writing at night how, 'after eighteen hours of work [...] my feet burn so much, it's as if they're in a fire.' Lorenzo too had lived 'by the sweat of his brow since he was a child.' He had to be endlessly resourceful to survive. Naturally, this sometimes entailed going slightly outside the law.

Lorenzo was born 'Perone' (with one 'r') at 28 Via Ospizio on Sunday 11 September 1904 at eleven in the morning, a time when the stomach starts to feel hunger pangs. The news was not considered of any importance in the local newspapers, except perhaps statistically: Lorenzo was one of the eight boys and five girls born in Fossano that week. His father Giuseppe – '27 years old, bricklayer' – went to the municipal register office the following day, bringing as a witness his brother Lorenzo – '23 years old, bricklayer.' Both signed their name 'Perrone', with two 'r's. The dialect surname 'Perùn' is pronounced in such a way that illiterate or semi-illiterate people frequently doubled the 'r' when spelling it. For some of Levi's aunts, the 'true' surname was without a shadow of a doubt 'Prùn'.

Lorenzo, who shared his name with his maternal grandfather and his uncle, who became his godfather at his christening the following day, would fall into the same error, signing himself 'Perrone'. Lorenzo did not progress beyond third grade at school, according to his record of employment (incidentally issued to Lorenzo 'Perone'). Although baptised, he wasn't religious, nor did he know the Gospel. He wrote with difficulty but walked a lot. His relatives testified in the Yad Vashem file that he had started working at the age of ten, presumably in 1914, at about the time the Great War broke out. We have no idea what he looked like during his childhood.

Lorenzo's brother Secondo would tell Levi's biographer, Ian Thomson, that Lorenzo was a 'born pessimist.'[26] It's all too easy to be influenced by hindsight. One of the last descriptions we have of Lorenzo is from a 1993 interview by Thomson with the former parish priest of Fossano, Don Carlo Lenta. In his last years Lorenzo sold scrap metal in the snow, 'without an overcoat, his face blue.'[27] It is certain than Lorenzo never learned how to forget, but there is no way of knowing if he already harboured anger and resentment at his lot in life by the age of ten.

CHAPTER 2

Knives and Curses

There is nothing romantic about the first photographic portrait of Lorenzo; in fact, it's quite austere. The photograph was taken during his military service in 1924–5. Lorenzo was serial number 29,439 and served as a *bersagliere* with the Seventh Brescia Regiment, today stationed in Puglia. Lorenzo enlisted (as 'Perone' with one 'r') on 25 April 1924, at the age of nineteen and was hospitalised less than three months later; no records have survived detailing why. He was finally discharged in October 1925 and returned home. 'During the time spent under arms his conduct was good, and he served loyally and honourably,' declared his captain.

In the two decades since Lorenzo's birth, Fossano had changed profoundly. The town's administration had overseen the introduction of electric light and the long-overdue provision of drinking water. The first stone had been laid for a new school. The paper and silk industries continued to have a strong presence in the area and the metallurgical industry grew from 1907 onwards. The first agitation for the improvement of working conditions, fair pay and trade union recognition also took place 1907. After the Great War, in which 312 citizens of Fossano died, there was a dramatic contraction in economic growth, as revealed by the local newspaper in 1918, when Lorenzo was fourteen: 'City life is a life of general idleness ... You may say: "but there are always people in the taverns and cafes!"

... But take a look at the work situation, at our industries: construction can be said to be dead and buried, in fact, bricklayers have had to change profession; and the effects of the crisis in construction are also felt by metalworkers, carpenters, tinsmiths, painters, etc. Not to mention the other professions: here too, times are equally lean.'[1]

Lorenzo Perrone in the military, 1924.

This was the context for the rise of Fascism in Italy: the so-called *biennio nero*, or 'two black years', which seemed to contemporaries like a state of civil war. The offensive against the working classes, soon supported by reactionary acts from the liberal State, industrialists, landowners, bourgeoisie and finally the monarchy, would prove deadly. In the first six months of 1921, for example, Fascists systematically destroyed trade union premises, left-wing clubs, popular cultural centres and so on: forty-nine such acts in Piedmont alone were recorded. On 4 May 1921 in the town of Mondovì, four Socialists were murdered by a

Fascist action squad; a similar event on 3 June in nearby Dronero saw the murders of two Socialists.

Angelo Suetta, a barber from Fossano, born in 1901 (three years before Lorenzo), would recall that on 1 May 1921, International Workers' Day, he had gone out 'from the Old Quarter towards Piazza Castello, where the trade union headquarters were, to join the parade ... but it was almost as if the city was under siege: Fascists, police and royal guards everywhere, armed to the teeth.' There had already been disorder and rioting and he had rushed to hide the register of workers who had joined the union.[2]

Lorenzo cannot have been unaware of this chronic political violence, which according to contemporary and later estimates claimed 3,000 lives throughout Italy. The Fascist seizure of power would lead to a process of 'normalisation'. This became obvious in Fossano after the removal of the Socialist militant Giovanni Germanetto at the end of 1922, followed by his arrest in spring 1923. In previous years Fossano's Santa Caterina prison had housed more than twenty Communists, Socialists and anarchists. As the 1930s came around, the warden, 'despite having investigated with "the greatest diligence", was unable to discover in the lists a single prisoner who had a record as having belonged to a Fascist squad.'[3] It is not hard to hypothesise what Lorenzo, eighteen at the time of the March on Rome, may have thought of his local community, where opponents and protesters ended up in jail, the Fascists circulated with impunity and the State did nothing to counter the systematic violence against workers and peasants.

Lorenzo was not a Fascist Party member, nor did he ever manifest any kind of support for the regime, to our knowledge. But peasants and workers too were attracted to Fascism; it was not only local elite and bourgeoisie. A stubborn dislike of the regime became endemic among the working classes, in particular those who crossed the border: in fact, they often migrated precisely because it had become increasingly difficult to find work in a Fascist city. But there is no documentary evidence to suggest that Lorenzo ever got into trouble because of political opposition to the Fascists. Nor does he appear among the 670 anti-Fascists who ended up in Santa Caterina during the twenty years of the regime, including such famous names as the Communist worker Remo Scappini, who would later lead the partisan uprising in Genoa in April 1945 and receive the surrender of a German general. Not that Lorenzo, who lived less than 200 metres from Santa Caterina, was no bother to his community. On the contrary.

...

Lorenzo got into fights, and likely relatively often, above all at the 'Pigher'. Rumours still circulate today in what remains of the *Burgué*. What emerges from the fading memories of the local community is that fighting may have been one of Lorenzo's main activities, or at any rate one of the most obvious, before his departure for Auschwitz. What remains obscure is how exactly these fights broke out. I have been unable to access any source that makes it possible to contextualise any of these episodes, and I have no idea how to do so, except by rooting though the memories of Lorenzo revealed by those who investigated his story *in loco* or through sources that bring us close to the context in which he lived. 'Being in conflict with someone ... was almost a state of mind, a modus vivendi that expressed a certain normality of relations, both between individuals and between communities,'[4] the scholar Alessandra Demichelis wrote. This partly helps us to bridge this gap in documentation.

In that province and at that time, there was 'excessive use of wine', which was considered a 'restorative nectar,'[5] and which gave rise to furious quarrels in which there was no shortage of sticks and knives. In that rural world, being 'ready' meant being 'responsive to arguments,'[6] and police raids were a frequent spectacle. Already by the beginning of the twentieth century, personal injuries, slanders, insults and drunkenness itself were among the most recurrent offences. This was a world 'filled with beggars, drunks, madmen, charlatans, swindlers, in which the weakest were doomed to succumb. Every village had its "idiot", derided and maltreated because of being mentally ill or simply "strange".'[7] As the historian and partisan writer Nuto Revelli writes, 'Within our valleys the unstable, the alcoholics, the misanthropes can be counted in their hundreds: a world that the healthy neglect or fear or despise.'[8] Such violence was apparent from the end of the Great War onwards, with increasing frequency. Firearms also made their appearance. It was a violent, brutal world, where man preyed on man: with or without a knife or stick. So though I think we can rule out the likelihood that Lorenzo owned a firearm, the men had to protect themselves. And sometimes, the best form of defence is attack.

The *Corriere Subalpino* put it this way in 1914, when Lorenzo was ten: 'Until a few years ago most of the common people believed in good faith that it was not possible to celebrate a country fair without the celebration being commemorated by blows being exchanged.' In these brawls, that involved kicking, punching, biting and beating with sticks; a particular excuse was not necessary. It was 'litigiousness widespread at all levels' for which 'any object within arm's reach could be turned into a weapon' (a bottle, stone, scythe or stick). Death was often only narrowly avoided.

> Alcohol and its abuse ... were ever present in the pages of the newspapers and in courtrooms. There was no secular or religious festival, ceremony or banquet that did not conclude with colossal drinking bouts, often followed by criminal acts. The tavern was the place of comfort and leisure where people sang, played cards or *morra*, and argued. Always drinking. Police reports provide calculations on the quantity of wine consumed, always litres per capita. All it took was one word too many, a barely tolerated nickname used with scorn, a disagreement over an unpaid debt.
>
> 'Oh Duro,' someone says in a tavern in Limone, the other person replies 'Oh Ver,'[9] and a violent brawl breaks out, with kicking, punching and stabbing. Crimes were committed inside the tavern but above all outside, once they had left or in the following few hours. Unconstrained and no longer lucid, people exploded in anger, even against those who might have been sitting at the same table just a few minutes earlier.
>
> [...] News items about fights that ended tragically are so numerous they cannot be counted, very many caused by the use of cold steel, especially knives with blades of a length that was not permitted. An inseparable companion, almost an extension of the hand of the farmer, the shepherds, the artisan, knives were so widespread that there were frequent attempts to regulate their possession and use, given the ease with which they were unsheathed.[10]

Historian Cesare Bermani, one of the pioneers of oral sources in historical practice in Italy, testifies the hypothesis that this *modus vivendi* was, as might have been predicted, often exported. The manager of a farm near Zossen in 1941 would note that the Italians 'always had a bludgeon within reach' when they worked, that they were 'undisciplined and insolent' and that a supervisor had been assaulted and punched in the face three times in a single day. The Italian émigré Gino Vermicelli, who went from France to Germany, would tell Bermani that 'the people who leave are always the most daring and unbiased, therefore also the most belligerent':

> Often they're also 'gangsters', in the sense that they're people who don't give a damn, because it's usually the Godfearing who stay at home, and it's of course these people who make most trouble, who work on the black market and so on. Anway these are the kinds of people who emigrate, some of whom may be pleasant and some not. Because in these emigrations you throw out the scum.[11]

If it weren't for the fact that it's difficult to think of Lorenzo as noisy and talkative, we could jump from the first decades of the twentieth century to the time of Lorenzo's 'homecoming'. In *The Truce,* Levi introduces the Moor of Verona, the elderly dormitory companion 'of more than human stature' with a 'deep chest [that] rose up like the sea swelling in a storm'. In the absence of a description of Lorenzo at the time, we have this image from Levi who knew Lorenzo so well. Here is the snapshot from the Moor of Verona's picaresque journey home:

He must have come from a stock tenaciously attached to the soil, for his real name was Avesani, and he came from Avesa, the launderers' quarter of Verona celebrated by Berto Barbarani. He was over seventy and showed all his years; he was a great gnarled old man with huge bones like a dinosaur, tall and upright on his haunches, still as strong as a horse, although age and fatigue had deprived his bony joints of their suppleness. His bald cranium, nobly convex, was encircled at its base with a crown of white hair; but his lean, wrinkled face was of a jaundice-like colour, while his eyes, beneath enormous brows like ferocious dogs lurking at the back of a den, flashed yellow and bloodshot.

In the Moor's chest, skeletal yet powerful, a gigantic but indeterminate anger raged ceaselessly; a senseless anger against everybody and everything, against the Russians and the Germans, against Italy and the Italians, against God and mankind, against himself and us, against day when it was day, and night when it was night, against his destiny and all destinies, against his trade, even though it was a trade that ran in his blood. He was a bricklayer; for fifty years, in Italy, America, France, then again in Italy, and finally in Germany, he had laid bricks, and every brick had been cemented with curses. He cursed continuously, but not mechanically; he cursed with method and care, acrimoniously, pausing to find the right word, frequently correcting himself and losing his temper when unable to find the word he wanted; then he cursed the curse that would not come.[12]

These are hints redolent of the rural areas of southern Europe, where wine, curses, knives and sticks were common; fragments of lives torn from the context in which Lorenzo was born and grew up, where he learned to grapple with life, and which he was able in some way to leave – and was not alone in doing so. They are images that belong partly to history, partly to hearsay, and partly to the myth of the 'good old days.' Do these fleeting yet concrete clues, comparable to Lorenzo's life story to a certain point, allow a glimpse of him? Can they fill the decades of silence – perhaps seasoned with curses – that he has left behind?

...

Although in the years of Fascism – between the violence of the early days and the 'normalisation' of the regime – Fossano had seen the growth of the dairy industry and an increase in the production of chemical fertilisers, and although the agricultural output of the surrounding area had increased in the 1930s, partly thanks to the regime's draconian decrees, this had had little effect, except superficially, on the massive flow of migrants. Migration had been omnipresent for centuries, but had intensified in the late nineteenth century, mainly as a seasonal movement, and become gradually more definitive in the period between the two World Wars. The people who thronged the border between Northwest Italy and Southeast France in the 1920s and 1930s were a lively and desperate bunch. For decades, that porous border had been crossed by shepherds and pedlars, by beggars who appeared at fairs with dancing marmots, by the *cavié* who bought and sold women's hair for Parisian wigmakers, by sellers of fireworks, woollen sweaters and canvases. The links between 'La Granda' – the province of Cuneo, of which Fossano is part – and Mediterranean and Alpine France is old and deep-rooted. In the first part of the twentieth century the disparity of needs and possibilities had become increasingly clear. There was a lack of bread in Italy and France needed manpower. Even the agricultural year was complementary: from November to March labourers were always needed in France to harvest olives, flowers, early fruit and vegetables for the grand hotels on the Côte d'Azur, and for the work of breaking and preparing the soil. When the cold weather arrived 'field hands, diggers, stonecutters, dock workers, porters', and with them many women, who went to work as maids and waitresses or to pick flowers or olives, 'went down' to France, most of them clandestinely.[13]

The temporary emigration of people from Cuneo drove workers to lead a life of struggle just to save something, and to swell the ranks of the 'Javanese', as the migrants from all over who flocked to Provence in the 1930s were generally called. In the 1939 novel *Les Javanais*, by Jean Malaquais (pseudonym of the Polish Jew Jan Malacki), the island of Java is vividly described as 'sunk in a concert all of its own, a concert of cantankerous voices, of oaths and moans.'[14] The Italians, in particular, were 'toads' – *babi* – in the eyes of many locals. In some places they were considered actual enemies, as the massacre in the Occitan village of Aigues-Mortes in 1893 demonstrated. There was narrow-mindedness and rejection in places, but there was also a genuine fusion in others. Even the early twentieth-century xenophobic novel *L'Invasion* by the prolific ultra-nationalist author Louis Bertrand, set in Marseille – just over 200 kilometres from Embrun – admits that the Provençals 'half' understood the Piedmontese,[15] of whom there were by now several thousand – though the novel generally oozes contempt for Italian immigrants.

Between the end of the nineteenth century and the era of Giolitti, the percentage of Piedmontese among Italian migrants grew by at least 1 per cent every year. Between 1916 and 1926, official numbers show 402,079 emigrants from Piedmont and Val d'Aosta, adding to the million and a half who had set off from the same regions in the previous forty years. Many of them went to the South of France. In some regions, there were almost forty times as many arrivals in the first decade after the First World War than there had been in 1916. This influx was picked up by alarmist paper articles in the late 1920s. By this time, Lorenzo was already twenty-three and had just finished his military service.

By the 1920s and 1930s, clandestine immigration to France had become a mass phenomenon. The Fascist regime had tried to put a brake on it, promoting exclusively temporary migration and suppressing the illegal kind. However, Fascist laws which, from 1927 onwards, aimed to restrict endemic immigration, only partly hampered the activities of the cross-border workers and resulted in the opposite effect. From the second half of the 1920s onwards, many migrants actually chose to settle in France permanently, despite inevitable tensions, 'assimilation was rapid and today the grandchildren of the Piedmontese immigrants are perfectly integrated and indistinguishable from the indigenous population. Often, they still live in the houses built by their grandparents. Travelling around the hills outside Nice, Cannes, Vallauris or the plain of Grasse, reading the names by the doorbells of the family houses, each with its own garden, most of the surnames are Piedmontese, especially from the province of Cuneo.'[16]

CHAPTER 3

And Night Came

Lorenzo, then, was certainly not the only man who spent as much time in France as in Italy, crossing the border in winter and returning in spring. Many stayed, becoming perhaps more French than anything else. By the middle of the 1940s there were 437,000 Italian workers in France, 120,000 of them in the construction industry, of which a high proportion were bricklayers and labourers. Counting their families and the many who had been naturalised French – no fewer than 150,000 by the beginning of the decade – we get close to a million Italians on French soil. It is unlikely that these people, who were primarily of working-class origin, were Fascists. But Lorenzo was imprisoned by the French authorities, on charges unknown.

There were a very large number of anti-Fascists in the Italo-French community. While insisting on the difficulty of making distinctions, the historian Cesare Bermani goes so far as to maintain that 'almost all the Italians in France [were] in a critical or hostile position towards Fascism,'[1] taking into account, among other things, that the political 'exiles' did not have a single unified organism of propaganda and were overwhelmingly working-class. The lives of these migrant workers had become more complicated due to their lukewarm or hostile attitude towards the regime that had caused them to migrate in the first place. A chaplain who worked with Italian agricultural workers in Upper Silesia and later in Austria would tell Bermani that 'anyone who leaves home often does so because they can't find work, and there may be various reasons, including politics.'[2]

The fact remains that in 1940 the Italians and the Italo-French, whatever their beliefs, officially became enemies. Italy had attacked France, crossing the Western Alps and delivering a stab in the back, a *coup de poignard dans le dos*, following the offensive by their Nazi allies.

After the war, another would begin for poor wretches like Lorenzo. Italians should have been making Italy great: that was the intention of those who were sending men to kill and die, first in France, then in Greece, Yugoslavia and the Soviet Union. Hundreds had left to fight the Duce's war from Fossano and even from the *Burgué*. The list of the fallen can still be found today behind the monument near the Bastione del Salice, which is all that remains of the city's sixteenth-century fortified wall.

It would prove to be a huge task – a needle in dozens of haystacks – to trace Lorenzo's presence in 1940 in the triangle between Nice, Toulon and Embrun – a perimeter of almost 400 kilometres. In an interview that appeared posthumously, Levi mentioned Lyons and Toulouse as possible sites where Lorenzo could have been living and working at the time, although he admitted he could not remember. Lorenzo was one of those thousands of people – no fewer than 8,500, according to what Levi and Angier were able to reconstruct – who had been imprisoned. When the stab in the back had been metaphorically delivered, the French defended themselves as one does when the enemy crosses the threshold of 'home' and one mistrusts everyone on the basis of the name they bear and the place they come from. While the Italians were suffering one of the most humiliating setbacks in their military history, Lorenzo held his breath. In jail, men with callused hands and feet almost always survive – at least he believed this to be true before 'Suiss' – and you even ate better than outside. But his respite from all that walking lasted only a few days. By the time the Nazis had overwhelmed France and taken Paris on 14 June, Lorenzo was released along with many of his comrades. This workforce became necessary to the economy of the Axis. By the beginning of July Lorenzo was definitely back in Fossano, at the employment exchange, asking for welfare. From now on, finding work in France would be more difficult for Lorenzo and other Italian workers like him.

In that region of fusion, the neighbour and the foreigner – the Italian – had now acquired the status of enemy, even in the eyes of the people. The border had hardened, turning literally into a front. Italians like Lorenzo, even when they were hostile to Fascism, had been born in the country of the future masters, who in the following years would occupy a large swathe of southern France, largely corresponding to the very areas in which he had worked. The Axis Alliance – Germany, Italy and Japan – wanted to conquer the world. They started with Europe, which they would reduce to rubble. But German, Italian and Japanese people still needed to eat. As Primo Levi has his alter ego Libertino Faussone say in *The Wrench*, 'a man learns late to say no to a job.'

Work at the time involved a lot of walking, whether or not you wore a uniform. There is no way of knowing how many times Lorenzo returned to France illegally in the early 1940s. Although I'm inclined to rule it out, it might actually have been from France that he set off, through the same channels – voluntary at first, then increasingly compulsory – that took thousands of Italian workers to Germany directly from French territory. The Fascist government exerted pressure to have Italian workers repatriated before being sent to the Third Reich, but their efforts proved futile. In whichever of the three territories – France, Italy and the Third Reich (i.e. Germany and its captured territories, including Poland) – a worker was hired, he would be working for the Axis anyway. Going back to Italy may have been risky for Lorenzo for another reason: men his age were being mobilised. In any case, some of the 178,674 workers who returned to Italy from France between 1937 and 1942 left again for Germany with collective fixed-term contracts. I assume Lorenzo was one of them.

As certified by Lorenzo's employment record, partly reproduced in the Yad Vashem file, Lorenzo came to Auschwitz with an Italian firm called G. Beotti. This employment sponsorship might have happened through an uncle who sent for him in Embrun, or else though his brother Giovanni. Primo Levi had been vaguer, writing in *Moments of Reprieve* that 'his choice had been anything but voluntary', because when the Germans arrived in France, after his brief internment, they 'had reconstituted the firm and transferred it part and parcel to Upper Silesia.'[3] Of course, it cannot be ruled out that this is what in fact happened, but Lorenzo's employment record reveals that just before he left for 'Suiss' he did over a month's work for a firm based in Tradate, a town in Varese, on a site in Levaldigi, a district of Savigliano still known today for the airport of the same name. At the time Lorenzo was working there, the area was expanding massively for military use, expropriating various properties in the area. The clients were in fact aeronautical companies.

Levi's words suggest that Lorenzo had undertaken the

quickest route, sparing himself at the very least some dozen kilometres on foot. And he was a man who walked a lot: apart from the constant to-ing and fro-ing across the border, we know for certain that in 1945 Lorenzo walked 1,412 kilometres in four or five months, following the railway line. But that's almost the end of the line, as far as this story is concerned, and to understand it we must take things in the right order and first get to know Lorenzo the way that Primo did.

...

'If a foreman made a remark about Lorenzo's work, even in the nicest way, he didn't say a word, put on his hat and left.'[4] This is how Levi recalled the years that preceded his own encounter with Lorenzo. This may be as Lorenzo himself told Levi, or Levi may have heard this from members of Lorenzo's family, who confirmed it to be true. It is perfectly plausible, given Lorenzo's well-known irascible character, although here it is given a perhaps idealised aura. From the formulation chosen by Levi, I hazard that this may have happened more than once between the middle of the 1930s and 17 April 1942, when at last Lorenzo reached the outskirts of Auschwitz. 'Buna', where he would work, was established in October that year, with the aim of producing synthetic rubber ('Buna' is the German nickname for Butadien-Natrium-Prozess) as well as synthetic benzine and colourants and other by-products of coal.

Lorenzo arrived at Camp Leonhard Haag, Lager I, where the Italians were housed. Today, the staff of the Auschwitz-Birkenau Memorial and Museum unofficially call the Italians *Ausweis*, to distinguish the *robotnicy cudzoziemscy* – the foreign workers – from the prisoners. Unlike the prisoners, foreign workers maintained their identities, with a document (an *Ausweis*) and a metal badge. A *Häftling* – prisoner – was recorded on a document (*Häftling-Personal-Karte*), which they did not keep with them.

Lorenzo's transfer to the part of Nazi-occupied Poland where Auschwitz was situated took place under the auspices of the Italian firm of G. Beotti. The three postcards sent from Polish territory by Lorenzo that remain, preserved in the Primo Levi Archive, bear the firm's letterhead.

It is impossible to tell during his time working in France whether Lorenzo was considered a simple bricklayer (*maçon*), a *terrassier*, who dug foundations on construction sites; a stone cutter (*tailleur de pierre*); or a *scieur de long*, a kind of woodcutter who operated in pairs, often working on railway sites. In Poland, according to the Arolsen Archives, which has preserved thirty million documents on seventeen and a half million people persecuted by the Nazis, Lorenzo's working title was simply *Maurer*, a bricklayer. The documentation that exists is plain and pitiless. The sources that have emerged give little sense of cause and effect, regardless of who produced them. All the documentation we can find about Lorenzo hovers impatiently, then converges at the moment of time, in the mid-1940s, when everything changed in a world at war, and when due to a complex combination of 'fortunate circumstances'[5] Lorenzo and Primo encountered one another.

Few people could have stood the pace that Lorenzo set, and not only when he walked over the mountains. His ability to keep going, to remain silent even when questioned, and to grasp the meaning of the things that matter, was formidable. Something good must have transmitted to Lorenzo, though he was cut from the same cloth as his father, Giuseppe

Perrone. Lorenzo finally came out from the war pure, marching stubbornly in the opposite direction down the road alongside the railway tracks that led to that place where 'men fell like insects', as described by Jean Gotfryd, a Polish Jew who survived Monowitz.

For 1,100,000 people, a number on which we cannot linger, else we stop here and the story ends as it ended for all those people – abruptly, in the first minutes, or the first days, or after a few weeks in the camp – for four out of five of those like Primo Levi, that road was one-way.

...

I assume that in his first months working in the camp, Lorenzo often gritted his teeth. There is no evidence that he got into any fights. He may have had 'a peevish personality'[6] according to his brother Secondo, but Lorenzo had no desire to tear things down. He was there to work, and work well done, and the dedication it entails, can intoxicate 'at least as much as alcohol,'[7] Primo Levi would say. Hard work and alcohol makes every human relationship difficult. There was no partner waiting for him at home – Lorenzo certainly never married, and there is not a single mention of a steady relationship. Until 1942 there was nothing that mattered more than building to Lorenzo, and the profound joy that Levi would describe in *Storie naturali* as 'the happiness of creating, of extracting something out of nothing, of seeing something new coming to birth in front of us, gradually or all of a sudden, as if by magic.'[8] Activity that teaches us 'to be whole, to think with our hands and with the entire body, to refuse to surrender to the negative days and [...] to know matter and confront it,'[9] but also a 'stupid honesty', if brought into the camp, because outside 'it is honest and logical to work'[10] whereas in a place where men are a silent herd in chains on the slippery slope to annihilation it isn't honest and logical at all.

In a tragic counterbalance to the work required of Lorenzo, Levi describes not the demonisation but the good that work leaves behind for those who do it in *The Wrench*. Work offers the 'pleasure of seeing your creature grow, beam after beam, bolt after bolt, solid, necessary, symmetrical, suited to its purpose; and when it's finished you look at it and you think that perhaps it will live longer than you, and perhaps it will be of use to someone you don't know, who doesn't know you. Maybe, as an old man you'll be able to come back and look at it, and it will seem beautiful, and it doesn't really matter so much that it will seem beautiful only to you and you can say to yourself "maybe another man wouldn't have brought it off".'[11] I doubt that Lorenzo saw it this way, when at last he reached Auschwitz, as a voluntary worker. Did he ponder over the compulsion that might be involved in building something that was part of the extermination machine? He would not return to admire it as an old man and his work at Auschwitz would not survive him.

...

1943 was a watershed year. Everything happened quickly that summer, from the fall of Fascism on 25 July to the announcement of the armistice on 8 September. The world as it was known, ended. Italy, which had launched on average one armed aggression every couple of years, pursuing military glory throughout Europe and beyond – Libya, East Africa, Spain, Albania, France, Greece, Yugoslavia and the Soviet Union – found itself with a war at home. The Italian Social Republic was born and the relentless depredations of the Nazis and their Fascist allies escalated. It was a 'brutal reawakening', Levi wrote, in which an 'enemy of violence'[12] like himself felt 'obliged to take action'[13] and became convinced of the 'necessity of an opposed violence.'[14]

Levi became a partisan. He was betrayed by a collaborator and captured on 13 December 1943, 'one spectral snowy dawn'[15] at the Ristoro di Amay Hotel in Valle d'Aosta. He was taken together with two Jewish women from Turin, Luciana Nissim and Vanda Maestro, lifelong friends of his – the latter also a chemist – and Aldo Piacenza. Levi was taken to Aosta, then transferred to the camp at Fossoli, from where he left for Auschwitz.

Who was Primo Levi at this time before he became the chemist, writer, witness, and above all the man, who everyone knows?

Several years ago, in 2010, there was an exhibition, curated by the historian Alessandra Chiappano and mounted first in Turin and then in Fossoli, called *This Time Was Given to Us by Lot*. It seemed to me to restore with uncommon force the story of a group of young Turinese Jews, some related. What emerged, corroborating the many pages devoted by Levi and by his biographers to the first nineteen years of his life, was an image of great humanity, friendship and – it sounds like blasphemy, but shouldn't – happiness. Sometimes photographs speak louder than words. There is one that captures Levi's great passion for mountaineering. It shows him in the mountains with four friends, among them Bianca Guidetti Serra (who wasn't Jewish) and Alberto Salmoni, who would survive the war and marry in May 1945. It is a snapshot of a radiant generation, later torn apart by Fascist violence, who matured in a few weeks 'more so than in the previous twenty years,'[16] as Levi wrote.

In addition to Levi, Nissim, Maestro, Guidetti Serra and Salmoni, this group of friends, all born between 1914 and 1920, included Emanuele Artom, Ada Della Torre, Eugenio Gentili Tedeschi, Franco Momigliano, Silvio Ortona, Franco Sacerdoti, Giorgio Segre and Lino Jona. Everything changed, shattered – although certainly not their bond – with the shame of the racial laws and then of their physical persecution. Of the Jews who remained in Italy, Della Torre, Gentili Tedeschi, Momigliano, Ortona, Salmoni and Segre escaped extermination; Jona died of tuberculosis in 1942 while bringing aid to foreign Jews interned in Astigiano, and Artom became a partisan and died horribly at the hands of the Fascists on 7 April 1944. While Primo Levi would survive, as would Luciana Nissim, two never returned from Auschwitz: Franco Sacerdoti, who was with Levi in Monowitz, then died during the evacuation of the camp, and Vanda Maestro, who travelled there with him. They had no way of knowing what was at the end of those interminable railway tracks – in fact, when Levi was captured, he actually declared himself an 'Italian citizen of Jewish race,' fearing that an admission of his political activities 'would have meant torture and certain death.'[17] But hope in salvation soon collapsed, in his experience and in his red-hot memory of those weeks as a prisoner. The pages of *If This Is A Man* are heartrending. With the aid of hindsight, Levi recalls how this conviction was deferred and the abyss opened wide in front of his and their eyes: 'Only a minority of ingenuous and deluded souls continued to hope. We others had often spoken with the Polish and Croat refugees and we knew what departure meant.'[18]

On Tuesday 22 February 1944, his journey of deportation began:

> And night came, and it was such a night that one knew that human eyes would not witness it and survive. Everyone felt this: not one of the guards, neither Italian nor German, had the courage to come and see what men do when they know they have to die.
>
> All took leave from life in the manner which most suited them. Some praying, some deliberately drunk, others lustfully intoxicated for the last time. But the mothers stayed up to prepare the food for the journey with tender care, and washed their children and packed the luggage; and at dawn the barbed wire was full of children's washing hung out in the wind to dry. Nor did they forget the diapers, the toys, the cushions and the hundred other small things which mothers remember and which children always need. Would you not do the same? If you and your child were going to be killed tomorrow, would you not give him to eat today?[19]

'Be a thief, it's much more honest,' Levi said scornfully to a policeman, before leaving. That journey would remain seared into his memory and into the memories of everyone who survived deportation. After five days suspended between life and death, he arrived in Auschwitz, at the age of twenty-four, twenty-two months after Lorenzo.

Levi saw a planet of 'phantoms'[20] who, like him, were 'frozen with terror' and 'grey and identical, small as ants, yet so huge as to reach up to the stars, bound one against the other, countless, covering the plain as far as the horizon.'[21] Dragged by force from their homes to work and die, or to work until they died, or simply to die, unceremoniously. They themselves were 'hunger, living hunger'[22] and this was all the doing of other human beings.

Without knowing it, Primo Levi was stepping onto the stage of history. Those months between the end of 1943 and 1945 made him one of the most distinct voices of the twentieth century. From Bolzano, from the train bound for Poland, he threw a note addressed to his friend Guidetti Serra, dated 23 February 1944, signed also on behalf of Vanda and Luciana. The note carried the words, 'We pass you the torch'.

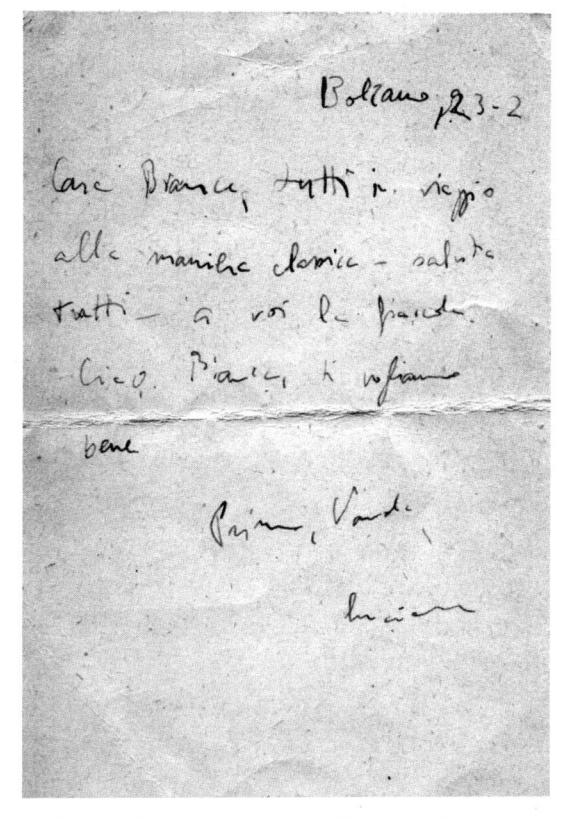

The note Primo Levi wrote to Bianca Guidetti Serra
while on the way to Auschwitz, February 1944.

Levi would survive, as we know, thanks to a delicate spider's web of sensible, decent gestures, and in the centre of that web was Lorenzo, for whom the precise order of events might have had little importance: for him 'time hardly mattered'. Levi himself would insist on this interpretation, declaring as early as in his first work, *If This Is A Man*: 'The story of my relationship with Lorenzo is both long and short, plain and enigmatic; it is the story of a time and condition now effaced from every present reality, and so I do not think it can be understood except in the manner in which we nowadays understand the events of legends or the remotest history.'

...

When he met Primo, two full years after arriving in 'Suiss', Lorenzo was about to turn forty, but with his body fatigued from manual labour and his hair already grey he probably looked older. He looked like his father, and an elderly father at that. This is the impression the reading of their first encounter on Polish soil suggests; an encounter between the 'Tacca', with his background of poverty, and the skinny young chemist, a mild bourgeois who had sunk into a situation of need.

It is worth considering how Levi would perceive forty-year-olds as witnesses and writers in his later life. In *If This Is A Man*, published in 1947, when he was twenty-eight, he tells of 'old Wertheimer' who, to escape the gas chamber, claimed he was forty-five, clearly making himself younger than he was. But the rest of Levi's work, published when he was between the ages of forty-four and sixty-seven, conveys a different feeling. In his 1982 resistance novel *If Not Now, When?* for example, we read that 'in wartime you grow old fast',[23] which is said of an Uzbek airman who has appeared from the bushes. 'He wasn't as young as he had looked in the snapshots' hanging in the fuselage of his downed plane: 'he must have been about forty.'[24] In *The Wrench* (1978) Faussone refers to a waitress who was 'about forty, bent and skinny'[25] and mentions the popular saying that life begins at forty. Without any claim to being exhaustive, Levi's output is filled with people who 'appear' about forty, one way or another; it is hard to say when these are considered old; what is certain is they are considered young only if at that age they die or are murdered or left to die. In *The Drowned and the Saved*, which Levi published not long before his own death, Guido Dalla Volta – the forty-five-year-old father of his inseparable friend Alberto – who died in the gas chamber in the great selection of October 1944, is described as 'old', with distressing quotation marks that represent the point of view of the Nazis.

We know what Lorenzo looked like in that period. Going by his passport, he didn't have grey hair in 1939, when news arrived of the war that was just then starting in Poland, or in 1940, when he had spent three or four days in a French prison. Did he suddenly age when he was declared unfit for duty and was unconditionally discharged from the army? Or when he reached the margins of Auschwitz in 1942?

...

When Lorenzo arrived in Auschwitz, in a place where every life was on the verge of sinking, all he had was his two-litre Alpine mess tin, which had been with him since his days in the 7th Brescia Regiment; a bit of cutlery, a grey-green cape, a much-patched sweater and a few other objects of no value. And he had in store a few words to be uttered with care.

These are the facts, mixed with legend, before history intervenes. Or perhaps what intervenes is our attempt to find something else that offers meaning and salvation in that 'time and condition now effaced from every present reality' – if that something exists.

PART II

You who live safe
In your warm houses
You who find, returning in the evening
Hot food and friendly faces:
Consider if this is a man
Who works in the mud
Who does not know peace
Who fights for a scrap of bread
Who dies because of a yes or a no.
— Primo Levi, *If This Is A Man*

CHAPTER 4

Wasting Away

In the end, and from the beginning, this is a story about human beings: their small-mindedness, their foolishness; but also their courage, capacity for being wonderful, even when they are cruel; and ability to keep on going, despite it all. At the same time, it is a story of apparently insignificant details that take on a vital significance, such as shoes. Shoes, as I came to realise during one of my many re-readings, may be the true protagonists of *If This Is A Man,* where they are present in sixteen chapters out of seventeen, and *The Truce.* Levi's work is strewn with references to how crucial it was, in the context in which Lorenzo met Primo, to be able to count on a decent pair of shoes. Up until a few days before his death, Levi never stopped insisting on the fact that shoes could determine your survival, 'down there': 'death begins with the shoes'[1] as it is bluntly put in *If This Is A Man.* Shoes were the final frontier: if well-made, they were on the feet of those who were free, like Lorenzo, or of those who commanded in the camp. The prisoners wore poorly made clogs called *Schuhe*. In the language of Auschwitz, a shoe was any object that managed to contain feet.

'They threw a pair of shoes on us; actually, not even a pair, two odd shoes, one with a heel and one without; you almost had to be an athlete to walk like that,' Levi recalled. 'One was too narrow and one too wide, you had to make complicated swaps, if you were lucky, and find a way to get two shoes that matched. But anyway, they were shoes that hurt your feet; anyone who had delicate skin on their feet would end up with infections.' It was already a brazen piece of good fortune to cross the threshold of the camp, it meant another day of survival. Of the 650 men, women, children and old people who had been loaded on Levi's train at dawn in February 1944, a morning that had come on them 'like a betrayer,'[2] just ninety-six entered Auschwitz. The others had been deliberately, immediately, murdered. And after the hailstorm of blows, being stripped naked, transformed into a herd and the other humiliations, for those ninety-six – who soon become ninety-five and then ninety-four and so on – a struggle for life had begun in which hunger, cold and work were the executioners. Those ninety-four, those ninety-three, like everyone in Auschwitz, died due to their shoes, as Levi pointed out.

> Anyone who was sensitive to infection *died of shoes*, of infected wounds to the feet that would not heal. The feet would swell, and the more they swelled, the more they rubbed against the inside of the shoes. You ended up going to the hospital; but in the hospital swollen feet weren't accepted as a disease. It was too common and anyone who had swollen feet would go to the gas chamber.[3]

...

It would be naive at the very least to expect a grand gesture on the part of Lorenzo or any other civilian worker. Keeping your head down was the only way to survive; the other route went from the margins straight to Hell. The same risk was run even by the civilians who worked in the vast area close to Auschwitz, but despite this there was no shortage of heroic gestures. Like that of the Polish peasant Wojciech Basik, from the mountain village of Korbielów, more than seventy kilometres from Monowitz, who, after encountering an escaped Czech Jew, Robert Wolf, in a railway station, hid him in his wagon, took him home and housed him in the barn. Basik took care of Wolf for seven months, without ever betraying him, despite the Gestapo's arrests and tortures by which they tried to extort a confession. Basik was given an award by the Czech government in 1964 and became a 'Righteous Among the Nations' in 1993. Wolf escaped in mid-July, about a month after the encounter between Lorenzo and Primo.

Although we shouldn't pass over such stories of escape and rebellion, in case there is any doubt, the margin for action was minimal for everyone – the workers who gravitated around the camp, civilians in the surrounding area, and the slave labourers themselves. There were still rebellions. The most famous took place in April 1943, when the last 60,000 Jews in the Warsaw Ghetto rose up heroically. The Nazis had exterminated almost half a million people confined there. Even the extermination camps saw regular uprisings, for example, in Treblinka on 2 August 1943, in Sobibor on 14 October 1943, and in Birkenau, seven kilometres from Monowitz, on 7 October 1944, when the men of the *Sonderkommando*, certain that the end was near, fought back against their oppressors. There were hundreds of escapes from the camps, which contributed towards leaking the first information on what was happening there. But, as Piotr M.A. Cywiński, director of the Auschwitz-Birkenau Museum – a giant of a man, both physically and intellectually, and capable of remarkable empathy – underlines, the Nazis had two powerful allies: hope of liberation, which the deportees never lost, and the family.

In the history of the Holocaust, Cywiński observes, whenever a revolt flared up, 'it was always in situations in which the family had ceased to exist, where people were risking only their own lives.' Normally, deportees wanted to stay with their loved ones right up to the end, 'supporting their elderly and sick parents,' helping their children get undressed, matching their shoes, calming them down. Few had the time or energy 'to offer resistance, to conspire, escape or fight. Entire families were murdered together.'

This should not be forgotten.

Still, tens of thousands of Jews joined the various European resistance movements. Levi dedicated his first and, strictly speaking, only novel, *If Not Now, When?* to them. These resistance movements were active from Western Europe to the north shore of the Mediterranean. Some of them even undertook major acts of sabotage. Among the best known are the Bielski brothers, who formed a partisan cell in the forests of Belarus. Their community protected one another and together, took up arms against their persecutors, and went into hiding, saving the lives of almost 1,200 people. It was an act of great defiance, which is indeed the title both of Nechama Tec's book about them and Edward Zwick's film adaptation.

When the world sinks into darkness – to echo the title of another book by Nechama Tec on Christians saving Jews in occupied Poland, *When Light Pierced the Darkness* – how can we break through it? Does success define the significance of our choices or can – should – we try at all costs, even if we know the resistance is doomed to fail? It's unlikely that Lorenzo asked himself these questions explicitly: when he met slave labourer number 174,517 he was one of the millions of workers tossed here and there in the darkness of Europe. He had no idea he was destined to live in the reflected light of that skinny man, not yet known to the world as Primo Levi. No one would have bet half a pint of dark wine in the 'Pigher' that Primo Levi would survive, let alone live to thank Lorenzo. What is certain, is what Lorenzo saw or at least intuited, as expressed by Levi in *If This Is A Man*:

> The personages in these pages are not men. Their humanity is buried, or they themselves have buried it, under an offence received or inflicted on someone else. The evil and insane SS men, the Kapos, the politicals, the criminals, the prominents, great and small, down to the indifferent slave *Häftlinge*, all the grades of the mad hierarchy created by the Germans paradoxically fraternized in a uniform internal desolation.

In that place which was 'the consecration of privilege and inequality', and of which Lorenzo had been granted a glimpse, did Levi already have 'the shame of the world'[4] and the shame 'of being a man'[5] written on his face? Because we are all made of the same petty stuff. To varying degrees, everyone was involved in the genocide.

A kind of unease penetrated the rough skin of this man who had grown old before his time, which overrode even the hunger that tormented Lorenzo day and night. Even with the pay the civilian workers received – not terrible, but less than a mark an hour (0.76 for bricklayers, between 0.56 and 0.62 for labourers) – he found himself stealing what he could to alleviate the pain in the stomach that never disappeared. Initially treated adequately, the Italian workers had seen their conditions deteriorate since the 'betrayal' of 1943 – as Polish historian Setkiewicz hints. Documents confirm that they had been going hungry even earlier: take, for example, the case of Giovanni Busicchia.

Busicchia, another labourer like Lorenzo, arrived at Auschwitz on 16 April 1942. He endured a month of extremely hard labour, receiving little to eat. After he was refused a medical examination despite his poor state of health, he ran away on 29 May 1942. He was captured in Villach and handed over to the Italian police, who imprisoned him for eighty days in Treviso, where he was from. Busicchia's prison medical report, made on 9 June 1942, found him to be 'wasting away, anaemic, with winged shoulder blades, a thoracic circumference of 72 centimetres and needing restorative energy treatment'.

Levi's plea for food was not articulated; it reached Lorenzo in different ways. Despite his own hunger, Lorenzo didn't hesitate. It was two or three days after their first encounter in June 1944 – enough time for him to arrange things – that Lorenzo came to work with his aluminium Alpine mess tin, which had been with him for so long. He held it out to Primo without saying a single word. Levi looked inside. It was full of soup, with salami rinds, salami and plum stones floating in it. Lorenzo told him to bring it back, empty, 'before evening.'

CHAPTER 5

The Language of Survival

Grey was the colour 'of the actions of people who want to survive and are prepared to make any compromise to do so,' according to Massimo Bucciantini. It was among the last things that Levi publicly investigated, in *The Drowned and the Saved*, after years of preparation. Grey was the colour of the Polish sky, even in summer; that mass of bloodied clogs and mismatched shoes sank into the mud; or the dust, amid rubble and bricks where not a single blade of grass grew. The winter of 1944 was the coldest of the century, with temperatures of twenty and thirty degrees below zero.

Today, if you visit Auschwitz at the end of winter or in spring, the greyness is hard to imagine. Auschwitz is – if I may be forgiven the blasphemy – a beautiful place, heartrending but wonderful. You may even glimpse fawns in the distance, as I did in 2010 or 2011, and the meadows of Birkenau, which have grown partly thanks to the ashes of hundreds of thousands of murders, were in flower. In the mild springs of the new millennium, nature is doing its best to stifle the most horrific manifestation of human culture.

The naked truth is that at the time, those untouchable *Häftlinge* ate everything that smelt of the life, before themselves becoming fertiliser. From dawn to dusk, exhausted as they were, they were allocated like pieces to Beotti and firms that collaborated with I.G. Farben, including Thyssen-Krupp, Daimler and Siemens. Initially used to actually build the

Lagers, prisoners were then systematically employed as slave labour by companies like those already mentioned, or DEST – *Deutsche Erd- und Steinwerke GmbH* – a firm owned by the SS. DEST operated in Mauthausen, producing material for the Third Reich's construction industry. Their turnover, thanks to slave labour, increased from 133,000 to 4,822,000 marks in five years. As the historian Gordon J. Horwitz demonstrates in *In the Shadow of Death,* a book concerning the complicity of the local population, that camp, like many others, did not spring up 'in a desert.' The first prisoners who arrived in Mauthausen, and who had had to walk across the city, 'retrace images of indifference: a man seen seating himself at the dinner table, a pair of lovers near the Danube.'[1]

When it was all over, in 1947, I.G. Farben – the company that brought Beotti to Poland – were put on trial in West Germany, in one of the twelve secondary trials at Nuremberg. In the 1960s, the German Democratic Republic held the same company responsible for the deaths of 75,000 people in Auschwitz.

The 'veterans' of the camp, including Primo Levi, were also a colour frighteningly similar to grey. To be alive five months after arrival was a challenge, considering that a human body needs at least 2,000 calories 'to survive in a condition of total repose.'[2] The food in 'Suiss' – if could be called food – provided about 1,600 calories, if you were lucky and didn't suffer thefts. You might survive with those 1,600 calories if you were lying down, but they certainly weren't 'enough to live on while working.'[3] 'This was the demolition of man; this is Fascism.'[4] The new Fascist society was built on piles of corpses and the shortage of calories was part of this infrastructure.

Primo shared everything with his inseparable friend Alberto Dalla Volta. Alberto was a stranger to envy, he was *joie de vivre*, and his presence brings a lightness to these pages imbued with the triumph of death and horror. So he had shared the two litres of soup gifted by Lorenzo, an extra portion each to top up the insulting slop that was distributed in Monowitz.

Soup ration distribution at Auschwitz III – Monowitz, early 1940s.

For Primo and Alberto, 'the bottom line is that that extra quart of soup helped to balance the daily calorie count.'[5] For both thin humans, the extra 400 or 500 calories Lorenzo's soup provided, though 'still insufficient for a man of medium build,'[6] gave un-hoped for energy. The two young-old men of the Lager, despite their relative expertise in the art of 'organising' (in other words increasing their own likelihood of survival, even by stealing) and feeding themselves, still gasped for breath like eels in the Stura trying to stay on the surface. In Lorenzo's soup they glimpsed the possibility that they might not die. That gesture of compassion was like a mouthful of oxygen when you have already lost hope of being able to resurface. Vital, and excruciating.

...

There is no point in hiding the fact that, when we write or read about the centre of the vortex of evil that is Auschwitz, we want to look away or take refuge in details that make it easier to bear. During the years when I began to feel an urgent, if occasionally fluctuating, desire to tell this story, I often needed a pause from the horror. The horror remained impossible to get used to. None of us can feel safe when we admit the extent of what human beings are collectively capable of; it shatters our belief in humanity. Once again, Primo Levi put it well: if we take 'a common sample of humanity'[7] and put it to the test, every day for months, if one person doesn't give way, another will. This is another reason why Lorenzo's 'plain and enigmatic' story is so important.

It's important insofar as it's a story of the margins of the Lager, about which very little has been written. Even though the margins partake of the same 'human condition, which is opposed to everything infinite,'[8] something distinct and immensely reassuring can be observed in that ground-level perspective that Lorenzo gives us. It is in the level of the 'clatter of ten thousand pairs of wooden shoes,'[9] mismatched, worn-out clogs that connected the world of phantoms and Lorenzo's own. Lorenzo was outside of it, it's true, but with hindsight we can make this observation that's equally true: he felt he *couldn't* be completely outside. I can't help imagining his solid legs shaking when Lorenzo realised he was 'on the threshold of the house of the dead,'[10] though he himself was alive. This story began in 1904 'at eleven in the morning' of 11 September with the birth of Lorenzo. But if he had not passed through what happened 'down there' in Auschwitz, his life would be recorded like so many others before him, buried in some archive, with no obvious significance. A few lines, something like:

> Lorenzo P., civilian worker for G. Beotti Company at Auschwitz-Monowitz, Katowice, Poland.

Instead, Lorenzo arrived at the place where people came to die of gas, hunger, cold, work and shoes, and reinvigorated an era, because, as the Talmud says, whoever saves a life saves the whole world.

...

Lorenzo didn't say exactly what Levi recorded he said in *Moments of Reprieve*: 'Oh well, what do you expect from people like this?' Five years later, a few months before he died, Levi presented this sentence in a more compact, more abrupt form, this time in Piedmontese dialect: '*Ah's capìs, cun gent' parei.*' ('Oh, of course, with people like this.') To which Levi said, 'But you're Italian', and Lorenzo replied '*S'capìs.*' ('Of course.') 'I never heard him speak Italian,' Lorenzo's niece Emma – Giovanna's daughter – who was about to turn seven at the time, told me,[11] confirming what her cousin Beppe had already told me two and a half years earlier.[12]

'*Ah's capìs, cun gent' parei*': this gives us an idea of how Lorenzo spoke, even when he was far from home. The occasions when he did speak were rare. In writing about Leonid, one of the protagonists of *If Not Now, When?* talks of 'a good boy with a nasty temper'[13] who stubbornly barricaded himself behind a silence that barely concealed anxiety. Levi was thinking of Lorenzo: 'He had tried several times to make Leonid talk. He had got some shreds from him, bits of a mosaic, to be reassembled patiently, like a puzzle, afterwards, the way you fit certain children's games together.'[14] In the same way, Levi tied to converse with Lorenzo, by virtue of his unique relationship with words.

Primo, unlike Lorenzo, was an elder child: he had a younger sister, Anna Maria. Unlike Lorenzo, he was not sparing with words, although he judged them for their intrinsic quality. 'Talker' would be one of his professions just as much as chemist, witness and writer were. 'I do not belong to the taciturn', he wrote, describing himself as one of 'those who speak' as opposed to 'those who remain silent.'[15] 'I am a talker. If my mouth were gagged, I would die,' he once said.

On his second profession, writer, Levi reflected a great deal, recognising in *The Wrench* that, like Tiresias, he had 'got involved with gods quarrelling among themselves,' and had received 'a strange power of speech,' which was an undoubted piece of luck and also a sentence, in some way. The risk of writing something that's 'botch, silly, unoriginal, incomplete, excessive, futile' is ever present for one who works with paper and language. Yet 'the profession of writing, because it grants (rarely, but it does grant) some moments of creation, like when current suddenly runs through a circuit that is turned off, and a light comes on or a rotor moves' 'can give fullness'[16] on good days just as much as manual work that is 'well done'.

Of those difficult and memorable days 'down there', between 1944 and 1945, Levi spoke even when he was preoccupied with the art of surviving. He did so because tomorrow we 'might be dead, or we might never see each other again', and so he clung to what matters, the things that make us humans, wavering towards good, steering clear of anyone who 'does evil for evil's sake.'[17] Primo Levi was convinced that to remain a man it was important to give voice to what man harbours in himself that is noble. And so poetry and prose, natural sciences, *savoir faire*, the desire to seek and discover the right word: all this and much else was for him a way of recouping more calories, of finding the hundreds he still needed in order to live. Though Levi needed calories, words were also crucial to his need to stay alive, especially as he had already risked losing them, first on the journey to the camp – 'we looked at each other without a word' – and then in the initial impact of Auschwitz. ('Then for the first time we became aware that our language lacks words to express this offence.')

Calories, words and a third element, luck, were crucial to Levi in staying alive: 'fortune' is the first noun that appears in *If This Is A Man*.

> I am a normal man with a good memory who fell into a maelstrom and got out of it more by luck than by virtue, and who from that time on has preserved a certain curiosity about maelstroms large and small, metaphorical and actual.

This description from the October 1986 preface to Levi's collected stories and essays – which appears on the home page of the Primo Levi Studies Centre website at the time of writing – reflects his relationship with memory, words and reality. In the same preface, he asks 'the reader not to go in search of messages. It's a word I hate because it causes me distress, because it makes me wear clothes that are not mine, but that belong to a human type that I mistrust: the prophet, the seer, the soothsayer.' Remarkable, coming from a man who for forty years worked with, and polished, words.

Of the many dissimilarities between Primo the firstborn who prioritised words and Lorenzo the second child who privileged action, the most obvious is their relationship with speech. 'If the Lagers had lasted longer, a new harsh language would have been born; and only this language could express what it means to toil the whole day in the wind, with the temperature below freezing, wearing only a shirt, underpants, cloth jacket and trousers, and in one's body nothing but weakness, hunger and knowledge of the end drawing nearer.'[18] It is not a question of value judgements: language shapes thought and reality is shaped by them, and can be a symptom of cruelty. The same is true of silence.

We have photographs that testify how Auschwitz looked but little to reflect on how it sounded. Above that din of clogs, terrible acts were committed in the most complete silence or, conversely, amid screams. Sometimes everything was 'as silent as an aquarium,'[19] sometimes the 'slaves of slaves' felt that they were in a hellish cacophony; each individual reckoning with their themselves. What mattered was one's relationship with power, however minimal and fleeting. With that relationship came the possibility of remaining rooted to one's own way of understanding the world, of clinging to the dignity of being alive, without others drowning in your place.

Primo Levi would absolve, 'all those whose concurrence in the guilt was minimal, and for whom coercion was of the highest degree'[20] quite 'light-heartedly' – both within Planet

Auschwitz and more generally as regards the destruction of the Jews of Europe. For a long time, beginning when he was still in the camp, he would search for the key to the problem of good and evil. Once past that first, traumatic moment, when Lorenzo said *'Ah's capis, cun gent' parei'* with a hint of ill-concealed revulsion, what happened later became clear to Levi, as far as the relationship between good and evil is concerned.

The truth – I am forced to cling to words, in this case to a word that's highly problematic – the truth is that everything we know about what developed in those six months 'down there' is raw material carefully worked over by Levi himself. I'm talking about the human relationship that grew from that handful of words, not about the *Burgué*, the life of the cross-border workers, Fossano in the twentieth century, the civilian workers in Auschwitz, the many 'truces', the homecomings, the nightmares that plagued night and day, the attempt to communicate pain. Primo and Lorenzo's relationship during those months remains enveloped in Levi's words, preserved *in vitro*. Nothing apart from these and a few collateral testimonies will bring it back to life. It was a relationship that swam against the tide. The camps were 'anticipations of the future'. 'If Fascism had prevailed, the whole of Europe would have been transformed into a complex system of forced labour camps and extermination camps' and 'we would find ourselves today in a world split in two, "we" masters on one side, all the others in their service or exterminated.'

Lorenzo – and who knows what role he would have had in that world – said little about any of this. How aware was he of the significance of his first gestures towards Primo Levi?

A remarkable novel set in Berlin in the 1930s, Ulrich Alexander Boschwitz's *Menschen neben dem Leben* captures the essence of a man like Lorenzo. Boschwitz was some ten years younger than Lorenzo and dead by the time Lorenzo had arrived in 'Suiss'. Here, Boschwitz describes an old beggar, Fundholz, who 'saw life every day for what it was and had no interest in seeing it for how it might be:'

> He was not cut out for being in company. Having to speak made him uncomfortable. To speak you had to think, and he had no desire to think. He was no longer accustomed to having thoughts or exploring problems, he made do with the bare necessities. Something to eat, money for a drink, a place to sleep.

The question must be asked, even if only in tribute to the immensity of this story and what message we take from it. Hindsight gives us a gently distorted image of that dark past and we know the outcome, which Levi and Lorenzo did not, at the time.

Had Lorenzo grasped that 'down there' it wasn't so much the present that was being played out as an image of the future? Was it that he 'detested Germany, the Germans, their food, their language, their war'[21] – as Levi would recall in *The Drowned and the Saved* – to such a point that he would risk everything just to help one man the Nazis had declared an enemy? Had he realised that, whether he was forgotten or remembered, celebrated or rejected, he would contribute to the writing of history well beyond his 'bare necessities'? Had he decided to throw a stone into the apparatus of extermination and communicate his mute anger from the margins? There were many ways to resist the masters. Nothing in the story of us humans is preordained. And Lorenzo, with his capacity for action, couldn't help knowing that one drop falling every day eventually becomes a tidal wave.

CHAPTER 6

Working in 'Suiss'

This story is still at ground level, perhaps because it's hard in the comfortable present to directly confront the desolate heath that is Auschwitz once again. So, yes, this is a story at ground level. It was 1944 and Primo Levi's shoes – if those 'enormous unpaired wooden shoes'[1] that he and others like him wore can even be called shoes – made him look like an old man. He clung to material objects to avoid collapsing, to avoid falling abruptly apart with every step as cheap shoes do. As he took special care not to trip over the shoes in front and to avoid having his own slipped off by those limping behind, his shoes – let's call them that for clarity's sake – faltered in the mud, negotiated cables and narrowly avoided the slimy puddles that hampered the pathways in the holes left by vanished flowers.

'Dripping and swaying'[2] like their owner, and like that herd of emaciated slaves who were marching with him, Levi's clogs were 'unbearably noisy, and encrusted with alternate layers'[3] of viscous mud and the machine grease which, in accordance with the camp's absurd regulations, had to be smeared on footwear every morning to shine it. Everyone had to be inspected, starting with their shoes, and the risk was considerable: there was no way to pass unobserved.

In the world outside, it's still quite common to judge people by what they wear on their feet. 'Down there' it wasn't so dissimilar. But the shoes worn by the slaves weren't a choice. They were made of worm-eaten wood, inadequate, incapable of carrying out thankless tasks or marching, working around the sun and the coming winter. The shoes were not made to fit, and ulcers and infected wounds they caused spread beyond their feet. Primo Levi himself no doubt considered it instructive, guided by his innate curiosity, to discover the importance of footwear in such a place. The first impact of the camp and its primitive clothing had been disturbing: he had been told to take off his shoes, taking care they weren't stolen. 'Stolen by whom? Why should our shoes be stolen?'[4] he had wondered in astonishment. He would soon discover it: only shoes like those of a priest, 'of extremely delicate leather,'[5] with a fabric of quality to ensure its traction and snugness, could defer the almost certain death that sooner or later awaited the herd of slaves. It was a brutal fact, in the upside-down reality of the Lager: anyone who didn't take care of his shoes was a 'fool'. 'To be without shoes' was 'a very serious fault.'[6] Having heavy, torn, unbecoming or even just dirty shores was hardly less so.

This was understood by each *Blockältester,* the person in charge of a hut, including Hut 48 where Primo Levi and Alberto were barely surviving. It was understood too by the Nazis, who weren't seen much in the Lager but watched the contagion of evil spread from section to section of the camp, from bunk to bunk. They understood it in their own humiliating way: the meaningless regulations in force in Buna prescribed that every morning the shoes, even those that were a pitiful sight and had already condemned their owner to death, should be 'greased and polished', even though there was no assignment of grease for this purpose. Money was of little use. Every evening each hut received 'an allocation of soup' which was 'somewhat higher than the total of the regulation rations.' The *Blockältester* would distribute the excess, using it mainly as 'gifts to his friends and proteges, then the recompense to the hut-sweepers, to the night-guards, to the lice-controllers, and to all other prominents and functionaries in the hut.' What was left over was traded for other 'acquisitions', notably the material for shining shoes. These disproportionate, ill-matched, foul-smelling clogs were regularly smeared with 'grease or machine-oil' or 'any blackish or greasy substance' that was 'considered suitable for the purpose' and which had been cleverly put aside in a mess tin. Each hut had its 'habitual supplier', who had 'been allotted a fixed daily recompense'[7] – provided that this guaranteed a constant supply of shoe grease. Because even though those who wore them had no right to life, the regulations cared a lot about shoes. What cruelty, and how human – just as everything in the Lager was human.

Levi would consider hate a 'bestial, crude'[8] sentiment. Even the word, legitimate in the context, which he uses dozens of times in his works, appears in *If This Is A Man* to indicate the attitude of the slaves not directed at the oppressors (let alone 'Germans'), but at the worksite. The very worksite where Lorenzo was working for the famous Beotti company from Piacenza:

> The Carbide Tower, which rises in the middle of Buna and whose top is rarely visible in the fog, was built by us. Its bricks were called *Ziegel, briques, tegula, cegli, kamenny, mattom, teglak*, and they were cemented by hate; hate and discord, like the Tower of Babel, and it is this that we call it: Babelturm, Bobelturm; and in it we hate the insane

dream of grandeur of our masters, their contempt for God and men, for us men.

...

Opening night is meant to take place in Prato, but because of the Florence floods of 4 November 1966, it moves to Turin. Among those in the audience in the Teatro Carignano are Lorenzo's sister Giovanna and her daughter Emma, who have been invited personally by Levi. The play is staged on 18 November, in Levi's home city. This dramatisation of *If This Is A Man*, adapted by Primo Levi with Pieralberto Marché (pseudonym of Pieralberto Marchesini) and presented as part of the 1966–7 season of Turin's Teatro Stabile, is the apotheosis of alter egos. Lorenzo changes name, becoming Pietro, and is played by the actor Pietro Nuti. Levi adopts for himself the pseudonym Aldo, also a chemist.

Einaudi published the playscript simultaneously as the show opened, with an introduction by Levi in which he explains that he has 'tried to preserve, for each character, its original human load, even though weary of the permanent conflict with the savage, inhuman environment of the camp.' In the show, as in the script, Levi gets Lorenzo to speak, to say things that we may assume Lorenzo reported to him later or that he did in fact utter, and which do not appear in either of the two editions (1947 and 1958) of *If This Is A Man* or in any other work of Levi's. These explosive words, for example:

ALDO What about your wife?

PIETRO I don't have one. (Pause). This world ... isn't right. I don't want to bring other poor wretches into the world.

ALDO So what are you living for?

PIETRO I never even asked to be born.

More than twenty years since the liberation, Lorenzo, who's been dead for more than a decade – acquires a new life. And, above all, speaks quite a lot. What follows is the moment in the show when Lorenzo/Pietro, comes onstage and has a dialogue with Aldo and with the tireless Alberto. After a while Elias Lindzin, the giant, another unforgettable character in *If This Is A Man,* passes by. Projected on the backdrop, part of the bombed worksite. Onstage, a wall under construction. A scaffolding made up of two tripods, with a plank across them as a bridge. On the scaffolding, Pietro with a darby and trowel. On the plank is a basin for the lime. Aldo come in from the right pushing a wheelbarrow with a shovel on it. He stops at the foot of the scaffolding. Pietro signals with a hand shaped like a shovel for him to lift the lime with the shovel and decant it into the bucket. Aldo looks at him, not quite understanding.

PIETRO *Los, aufheben.*

Aldo takes the shovel and plunges it clumsily into the lime.

ALBERTO (*enters left, pushing a wheelbarrow, sees Aldo and stops beside him for a moment*) Ah, so they've got you doing manual labour now? But that's not how you do it. There. (*Showing him*) You see?

PIETRO So you're Italians?

ALBERTO (*to Aldo*) For God's sake, you have all the luck. An Italian bricklayer. Don't waste the opportunity, for fuck's sake! That one over there's waiting for me with the wheelbarrow.

(*He goes off, though turning his head to look back*)

PIETRO It's obvious you're not in the trade. But the work still has to be done. (*He looks around cautiously, then comes down slowly from the platform*) Let me. (*Decants some shovelfuls of lime from the wheelbarrow into the bucket, then hands the shovel back to Aldo*) There, now pretend to carry on. (*Climbs back up and sets about rendering the wall*).

ALDO (*stands there dazed for a few moments, then, quietly and with a degree of embarrassment*) Thank you. (*Pietro continues his work without replying*). Where are you from?

PIETRO (*unhurriedly*) Fossano.

ALDO Why are you here?

PIETRO (*shrugs, then, phlegmatically*) I'm a volunteer. They sent me to Germany as a volunteer.

ALDO How do you mean, a volunteer? Did you want to come or didn't you?

PIETRO You know how it is, we bricklayers go all over the world. I was in France, with a company; the Germans came and brought us here. (*Shrugging again*) I'm a volunteer …

ALDO How do you manage?

PIETRO One workplace is as good as another. Not much bread, lots of potatoes, no wine. We're in a hut: on Sundays we have the day off. Like in military service. Not like you people.

ELIAS (*moves from right to left with a sack on his back: he puts the sack down for a moment and looks at the two of them working*) Qué bueno este italiano! (*Joining the index fingers of his two hands, allusively*) Combinazia! (*He picks up his sack again and exits*).

ALDO I'm from Turin ... For us it's different.

PIETRO (*looking around cautiously and speaking warily*) Yes, I know. But these people don't know anything: I've seen what they do to you ... (*Pause, then continuing to work*) And the road to Birkenau ... (*Another pause*) I've never studied, but as far as I'm concerned, a Jew is as good as any Christian. (*Pause. Continues working*) It's best we come to an agreement right now because we're like birds of passage here. We're working here today, tomorrow who knows? Every morning, after the second siren goes, come to the big woodpile. You know where that is, don't you? Facing Hut 930, on the corner of H-Strasse. Bring an empty mess tin: you'll find a new one. Try not to be seen. But I don't need to tell you that ... That's a job you all know how to do.

ALDO What about you, won't you be there?

PIETRO I shouldn't be seen either. You know what they'll do to us if they catch us together outside work: you go to the gas chamber, I get put in the Lager, like you lot.

ALDO Let's get to the point. Nobody takes risks for nothing. I have nothing to give you, not here. Perhaps in Italy, later, if I get out of this.

PIETRO What are you talking about? I didn't ask for anything. When something needs doing, you do it. (*Comes down from the bridge and looks at a wall, closing one eye to check if it's straight*)

ALDO (*almost laughing*) Like building a wall.

PIETRO (*serious, not picking up on the humour*) That's right. (*Climbs back up to smooth the plaster*)

PART III

Instead, in a voice so calm it surprised even him, he said: 'Of course, it wasn't an easy choice for me either; but I believe it's the best. A man has to weigh his choices carefully.' And he added meaningfully 'and also his words'. Leonid didn't answer.
— Primo Levi, *If Not Now, When?*

CHAPTER 7

Messages

'Volunteer. They sent me to Germany as a volunteer,' says the bricklayer Pietro in the stage version of *If This Is A Man*, a self-contradictory formulation that somewhat negates the concept of volunteering. 'Did you want to come or didn't you?' a mildly impatient Aldo presses him. Pietro's answers are wise, Sybilline, laconic, implying perhaps that 'down there' in the arsehole of the world (Levi's *anus mundi*), in a context of 'not much bread, lots of potatoes, no wine', there weren't really all that many volunteers: the meals mentioned on his personal canteen card confirm that the wretched 'menu' was basically bread and soup.

Where I've spoken about 'volunteers' in this book, I've put the words in quotation marks, as Levi himself did later in life. There must have been a constant sense of compulsion to work between 1943 and the early summer of 1944. By August of that year, it is estimated that there were 7,651,970 foreign workers, civilians and prisoners combined (prisoners being a quarter of the workforce) in Germany. A few months earlier, the *Gauleiter* of Thuringia, Fritz Sauckel, had declared that 'of the five million foreign workers who came to Germany, not even 200,000 came voluntarily.' In Lorenzo's hometown of Fossano, for example, the Fascist leaders looked for their 'volunteers' among the 'idlers' and 'ex-soldiers'. It was not at all easy to find people willing to leave and non-compliance could be harshly punished. Only a few tens of thousands of the 82,517 Italian workers who left for the Reich after 8 September 1943 could be considered 'volunteers': 'The quotation marks are indispensable', historian Bermani writes.[1] In this 'vast and complex' world of exploitation, the first Italians to be recruited, having been prevented from returning to Italy, assumed a role 'halfway between a hostage and a forced labourer,' historian Mantelli revealed in his study *Camerati del lavoro*. About 100,000 thus remained trapped in the Third Reich. In Monowitz, between Auschwitz III and the I.G. Farben factories, there seem to have been 30,539 slave workers during this same period, mixed in among almost 80,000 other people – of which about 35,000 were civilian workers of various nationalities and about 1,000 were British prisoners of war. The Italian civilian workers were hard to distinguish, in terms of conditions, from the forced labourers. Their situation has been reconstructed recently by the historian Laura Fontana in *Gli italiani ad Auschwitz*, an exhaustive work published by the Auschwitz-Birkenau Museum, which devotes a chapter to the civilian workers and a few pages to Lorenzo. Some workers, as revealed by the Arolsen Archives, were hired directly by I.G. Farben.

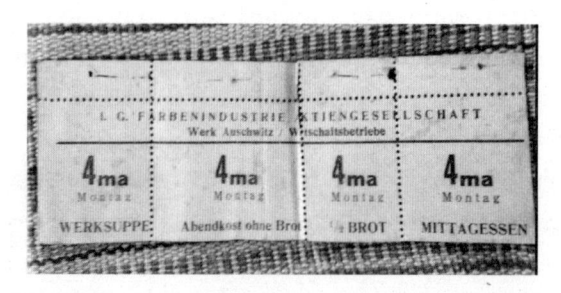

Lorenzo Perrone's food stamps from Monowitz (the Buna),
the I.G. Farben camp-factory, 1944.

Such is the case with Pietro Cademartiri, a bricklayer from Piacenza, ten years younger than Lorenzo.

In any case, as the months went by, whether they signed on of their own free will, like Lorenzo, or were more forcibly recruited, the 'free' workers of Monowitz, found themselves in some difficulty. In his highly detailed work on the history of the camp, the Polish historian Setkiewicz recounts how their work conditions soon became much more unpleasant than those promised by the recruiters, with the effect of creating, for example among the French, a gridlock of 'volunteer' workers who reported sick. Some attempted to escape, with one notable success: Belgian ex-civilian worker escaped from Monowitz and reached Great Britain, where he supplied Allied intelligence with information that made it possible for the complex to be bombed in the second half of 1944.

The Italian workers were treated decently at first, but their condition worsened in 1943, even though the documents do not point to any particular persecution or discrimination. If it is true that refusing to work could lead to arrest or repatriation in order to deter other foreigners, trying to help the prisoners of the concentration camp was quite another matter. It isn't clear how explicit this was – or how frequent – but it's obvious that even just imagining you could end up 'on the other side' was a powerful deterrent. Not for Lorenzo, of course, because 'when something needs doing, you do it.'

After their first encounter amid the rubble in June 1944, Lorenzo brought Primo and Alberto food every day. From that moment on, 'there always was soup, sometimes accompanied by a slice of bread', Levi would recall; 'as long as I was working as his helper, the delivery encountered no difficulty, but after a couple of weeks he (or I – I can't remember) was transferred to another corner of the work grounds, and then the danger increased.'

> The danger was for us to be seen together: the Gestapo had eyes everywhere and any one of us seen talking with a 'civilian' for reasons not justified by work risked being tried for espionage. Actually, the Gestapo had other fears: they feared that the secret of the Birkenau gas chambers would leak into the outside world through the civilian workers. Also the civilian workers ran a risk: whoever among them proved guilty of illegal contacts with us ended up in our Camp. Not indefinitely like us; temporarily, for a few months, for the purpose of Umschulung: re-education. I myself made a point of warning Lorenzo of this danger, but he shrugged his shoulders without a word.[2]

Lorenzo was the one who risked the most – 'you know what they'll do to us if they catch us together outside work: you go to the gas chamber, I get put in the Lager, like you people,' as he says in the stage adaptation of *If This Is A Man*. Yet to guarantee the two men those vital calories, Lorenzo did the rounds of the dormitory every evening to collect leftovers from among his companions, telling them there were two Italians among the Jews in Auschwitz. That's why the soup was somewhat unusual: once, Primo and Lorenzo even found in it 'the wing of a sparrow with all its feathers', another time, 'a scrap of Italian newspaper', as Levi wrote.[3] In the TV programme *Il coraggio and la pietà*, he even told Nicola Caracciolo which newspaper had been 'cooked': *La Stampa*, the daily from his hometown of Turin.

Levi would express his gratitude to Lorenzo's colleagues: 'They too were hungry, even if not as hungry as we, and many managed to do a little private cooking, with stuff stolen in the fields or found by scouting around.'[4] As time passed, unaware – as far as we know – of the immense dangers he was running, Lorenzo refined the art of making do for other people, filching 'directly from his camp kitchen what was left in the cauldrons, but in order to do so he had to go into the kitchen on the sly, when everyone was asleep at three o'clock in the morning.'[5] This cooperation in the attempt to save Primo and Alberto led Levi and Lorenzo to devise a plan. 'To avoid being seen together, we decided that upon arriving at his place of work in the morning Lorenzo would leave the mess tin in an agreed-upon hiding place under a pile of boards. This arrangement worked for a few weeks.'[6]

Before long, Lorenzo was supplying so much that Primo and Alberto had the problem of how to transport this extra food, as Levi recounts in *If This Is A Man*:

> To solve the problem of transport, we had to procure what is called a 'menaschka' here, that is, a zinc-pot, made to order, more like a bucket than a pot. Silberlust, the tinsmith, made it for us from two scraps of a gutter in exchange for three rations of bread; it was a splendid, sturdy, capacious pitcher, with the characteristic shape of a neolithic tool.
>
> In the whole camp there are only a few Greeks who have a menaschka larger than ours. Besides the material advantages, it carries with it a perceptible improvement in our social standing. A menaschka like ours is a diploma of nobility, a heraldic emblem: Henri is becoming our friend and speaks to us on equal terms; L. has assumed

a paternal and condescending air; as for Elias, he is perpetually at our side, and although he spies on us with tenacity to discover the secret of our 'organtsacja' he overwhelms us at the same time with comprehensible declarations of solidarity and affection, and deafens us with a litany of portentous obscenities and oaths in Italian and French which he learnt somewhere and by which he obviously means to honour us.[7]

In this story of men brought face to face with their own mortality, reduced by the pitiless hierarchies of the Lager to a purely physical condition, we still need to return to the deep meaning of these gestures – gestures repeated with impressive commitment, as if we were in another place, a place where humanity was granted some space, however minimal. In the famous chapter of *The Drowned and the Saved* dedicated to the 'grey zone', Levi would describe the devastating impact of entering the 'upside-down' world of the Lager:

> Instead, the arrival in the Lager was indeed a shock because of the surprise it entailed. The world into which one was precipitated was terrible, yes, but also indecipherable: it did not conform to any model, the enemy was all around but also inside, the 'we' lost its limits, the contenders were not two, one could not discern a single frontier bur rather many confused, perhaps innumerable frontiers, which stretched between each of us. One entered hoping at least for the solidarity of one's companions in misfortune, but the hoped-for allies, except in special cases, were not there; there were instead a thousand sealed-off monads, and in between them a desperate and continuous struggle.

> This brusque revelation, which became manifest from the very first hours of imprisonment, often in the instant form of a concentric aggression on the part of those in whom one hoped to find future allies, was so harsh as to cause the immediate collapse of one's capacity to resist. For many it was lethal, indirectly or even directly: it is difficult to defend oneself against a blow for which one is not prepared.[8]

In a kind of mirror image, it's as if the presence of Lorenzo straightened him up again, or at least contributed to his not completely falling apart. And this is the closest thing we can find to a paradox. Here was a man who had grown up – and grown old – in a wretched, aggressive world. Lorenzo got by in a context of hardship, dodging the blows that reality unleashes on the stooped backs of those forced to work hard. He had all the characteristics of a man of few words and much resentment, who might have leapt at the chance to get his own back on someone who is underneath, over whom he could exercise power. Shortly before his death, Levi expressed the rule, 'privilege, by definition, defends and protects privilege.'[9] And yet this was a man who spat on that privilege. The irascible, quick-tempered bricklayer Lorenzo, who had every reason to turn away these two people, instead endowed them with a good luck he could never have dreamed of receiving himself.

I don't know if this is a 'message' – I am trying to remain within the lines traced by Levi. Levi shares his thinking explicitly in 'Lorenzo's Return', as he retraces the events of that summer, soon to fade into a frozen autumn:

> Alberto and I were amazed by Lorenzo. In the violent

and degraded environment of Auschwitz, a man helping other men out of pure altruism was incomprehensible, alien, like a saviour who's come from heaven. But he was a morose saviour, with whom it was difficult to communicate. I offered to have some money sent to his sister, who lived in Italy, in exchange for what he did for us, but he refused to give us her address.

Every time I read these words something shatters inside me. To think that the world was and, all too often, still is obscenely unjust, but that if we look closely, in every abyss of pain and oppression, there is one who is just and transparent.

...

I have broadly introduced the only significant parts of Levi's memory that pertain to how Lorenzo looked and what he said during these episodes. Between 1947 and 1981, apart from the name he is given in the dramatization of *If This Is A Man*, Lorenzo always appears under his real name in Levi's testimony. During a conversation in November 1976 Levi said, 'Ah, Lorenzo, I called him Antonio', with reference to Saint Anthony, who fed the hungry.

As for Lorenzo's physical appearance, we shall see later how it was recorded by Italian bureaucracy between the 1920s and the early 1940s. Levi does not describe him in either of the two editions (1947 and 1958) of *If This Is A Man*; it was only when Levi was over sixty that he would sketch a portrait of Lorenzo. In 'Lorenzo's Return', published in the 1981 collection *Moments of Reprieve*, the bricklayer is 'tall, a bit stooped, with grey hair.'[10] Five years later, in *The Drowned and the Saved*, he becomes 'an old, almost illiterate bricklayer.' What remains somewhat mysterious is the process by which, in this last book published in Levi's lifetime, Lorenzo loses his name – perhaps because he is the bearer of a universal 'message', or because by now his name is connected with Levi's children? – and becomes irreparably 'old' in memory. Memory being a 'marvellous but fallacious instrument,'[11] we can't conclude that his memory of Lorenzo has been diluted. As he refers back to the two previous texts, perhaps he didn't want to repeat himself.

...

Very few of Lorenzo's words have reached us. Those first words – 'Oh well, what do you expect from people like this?' *'Ah's capis, cun gent' parei'* – are Lorenzo's only words in the texts published by Levi between 1947 and 1986. Others can be retraced, for example those few included in the explosive dialogue reported by Levi in a TV interview not long before he died, and which we have already cited: 'And I said to him: "You're taking a big risk, talking to me." And he said: "I really don't care."' Or these other words that we find in the transcript of the same interview, where Levi remembers saying, 'Careful, it's dangerous, you'll get into trouble', and Lorenzo replying, 'I don't give a damn.'

Many words, as we have seen, appear in the stage version of *If This Is A Man*, where a Pietro free to dare (perhaps because he now has a pseudonym?) talks a lot. Above all, about his work. The dialogue continues:

ALDO (*surprised*) Do you like working?

PIETRO At my age, there's nothing else you're fit for. And anyway, it's not a bad profession. (*With a touch of pride*) Putting up a vaulted ceiling! Not many can do that these days. The castle at Stupinigi, the restorations, I worked on that too. And also in France, that other big castle, by the sea.

ALDO What castle?

PIETRO I remember it well. I went there in winter, when there was no work at home. (*Pause, then, remembering*) In Toulon. I went there on foot, without papers, in secret. Seven days, quite a walk.

Punctuated by his reflections on the world that 'isn't right' and on the fact that he 'never asked' to be born, Pietro/Lorenzo accompanies his actions with words, emphasising their significance. 'When you're there, you have to stay there. You have to do the best work you can, and if it's impossible, do a little good,' he maintains prosaically. 'A little good, here in Auschwitz?' Aldo/Primo asks in astonishment, perhaps incredulous. 'Precisely. There's plenty of opportunity,' the bricklayer replies curtly, before getting down off the platform and looking with satisfaction at his work. These pages, then, contain an explicit verbalisation of his acts by this 'almost illiterate' and 'almost uneducated' bricklayer. The language is blunt, the content clear. In Auschwitz, 'you did what you could,' just as you did in Fossano earlier in the century, when Lorenzo was growing up. In practical terms, this meant that every evening Lorenzo brought the two veterans of the Lager 'six or eight pints of soup from the Italian civilian workers'[12] – a treasure of inestimable value. To get by, the slaves of the slaves had to 'get busy, organise illegal food, dodge work, find influential friends, hide one's thoughts, steal and lie,' because 'whoever did not do so was soon dead.'[13] Lorenzo, a 'free' worker, thought about his jobs and about how to help, according to the circumstances. *Remembering Survival: Inside a Nazi Slave-Labor Camp* by the historian Christopher R. Browning offers an investigation of the Nazi labour camp of Starachowice and who was responsible for the crimes committed there. It tries to define the 'moral system' in vogue among those slave workers, some of whom ended up in Auschwitz. A system based on 'a hierarchy of moral obligation rather than either an impossible universality or a total annulment of moral obligation': not an 'uninhibited assertion of self-interest'[14] but an evaluation of the circumstances, on a case-by-case basis. Clearly this is what Lorenzo did, without much splitting of hairs, even after fate distanced him from Primo (it was he who was transferred, not Levi). It was a moving counterbalance – six or eight pints every evening! – to what was a (paradoxically) almost brutal attitude among the civilian workers: the fact that the slaves were '*Kazett*, a singular neuter word', 'does not stop many of them throwing us a piece of bread or a potato now and again, or giving us their bowls, after the distribution of the "*Zivilsuppe*" in the work-yards, to scrape and give back washed':

> They do it to get rid of some importunate starved look, or through a momentary impulse of humanity, or through simple curiosity to see us running from all sides to fight each other for the scrap, bestially and without restraint, until the strongest one gobbles it up, whereupon all the others limp away, frustrated.[15]

There was no lack of 'opportunities' to do good in Auschwitz, says the bricklayer, who already at the time of the events must have had, in a narrow sense, an overall vision. Since the Italian workers' camp was situated on a hill that 'looked down on the smoking chimneys of Birkenau on one side, and the living dead of Monowitz on the other,' as Angier observes, he and his colleagues 'understood exactly what was happening; and suffered accordingly.'[16] On clear days – this would remain imprinted in Levi's memory – you could see 'the flames of the crematorium'[17] from Buna. This is how, in 1978, Deichmann, the director of I.G. Farben for Italy, described the view bricklayers like Lorenzo had: 'the Italian construction workers were housed in a shanty town built on a little hill with a panoramic view over the whole of the vast worksite and, on the other side, over the extermination camp, which, wrapped in the mist and smoke of its sinister chimney stack, looked like Hell itself.'[18] So Lorenzo observed, made a rapid judgement and took concrete action, taking as much care as he could because the spot they had agreed on for the regular handover of food was not far from the Italian Work Office (*Italienisches Syndikats-Büro*), which 'teemed with spies', according to Thomson.

Levi's memory is infallible when it comes to talking about Lorenzo's actions, enumerating them in *If This Is A Man* and returning to them in *Moments of Reprieve*. Because in the end, what matters is what we do. This isn't just an old adage, but a prominent factor in much of Levi's writing. The value of a man 'depends on what you want from him,'[19] says the watchmaker Mendel, the protagonist of *If Not Now, When?* (into whom Levi 'put much of himself'[20]) but above all on how he behaves. Miranda, a character from the science fiction story 'Psycophant' says that 'what counts is what one does, not what one is. One is one's actions, past and present: nothing else.'[21] And although this is an ironic, humorous story, the friends Miranda addresses in these pages were, as Bianca Guidetti Serra would recall, basically Levi's old circle of friends; 'all of us, but perhaps especially those of a certain group that had its roots in 1938 – the time of the racial laws that imposed, even on non-Jews, an unavoidable choosing of sides – and which from that point on continued to flourish.'[22]

Perhaps the most surprising fact is that Lorenzo – who clearly chose his side – didn't merely sustain Primo in his vital, primary needs but went further. I've mentioned the fact that the name of the Piacenza-based firm of G. Beotti for which Lorenzo worked can be found on the postcards sent by him, preserved at the Primo Levi Archive. Many other Italian civilian workers on the edges of Auschwitz wrote home, as reconstructed by Laura Fontana thanks to the Arolsen Archives (most of the thirty million documents have, incredibly, been put online) and to various fortuitous circumstances that have made it possible to track down an infinitesimal fraction of them. Some of these writings have appeared in the last few years on eBay. Others, thousands perhaps, or even hundreds of thousands, remain in the archives or in cellars across Europe. In any case, the workers serving the Reich, those who were more or less literate, did communicate with their nearest and dearest. To take two examples, the Friulan bricklayer Pietro Lusa, five years younger than Lorenzo and hired by the firm of Pagani, sent his wife Giuseppina a twelve-line postcard in which he reassured her twice about his state of health, giving rise to legitimate suspicions that he wasn't well at all; and the

Paduan assistant mechanic Bruno Mioni, who was the same age as Levi, confessed to his father Umberto, at about the same time as Primo and Lorenzo met for the first time, that he was 'very sad' and felt 'very homesick for my house, my family and my land.' And yet, as far as I know, Lorenzo never wrote home, not even to let them know how he was. Perhaps it was because 'these were times in which even hope could be frightening,' as Guidetti Serra would remark laconically in her memoirs, *Bianca la rossa*. There is no trace of a postcard from Lorenzo to his parents – both still alive at the time – or to his brothers or sisters, not a hint in the memories of the family, as they've been handed down to us, or as I've had the chance to investigate personally. What makes this all the more interesting is that Lorenzo did write postcards, but he wrote them for Primo, after the latter, having been discovered, failed in the attempt to write one himself.

Levi tells the story in 'A Disciple', from *Moments of Reprieve*. 'In June [1944], with frightful irresponsibility, and through the mediation of a "free" Italian labourer who was a bricklayer, I had written a message for my mother, who was hidden in Italy', actually addressing it to Bianca; 'I had done all this as one observes a ritual, without really hoping for success.'[23] And the postcard, in surprisingly neat handwriting, reached its destination.

...

Among the acts attributable to Lorenzo, this one in particular stands out. Perrone (with two *r*s) did not exploit the postcard-writing privilege for himself, but for someone else. He didn't simply recopy, and he didn't hesitate to describe himself as 'his friend'. We have no way of knowing

MESSAGES

> 25.6.44
>
> Carissima signorina Bianca
> o visto ieri primo sta
> bene lavora e forse le
> scrivera e un po dimagrito
> e attende di rivederti
> o almeno le tue notizie
> Qui cè niente di nuovo
> molti ringraziamenti da
> parte sua e tanti saluti
> lo. Pe. e sono il
> suo amico Perrone
> Lorenzo.
> spero di ricevere
> un suo scritto
> addio

The first of Primo Levi's letters sent by Lorenzo Perrone
from Auschwitz, 25 June 1944.

how much a gesture like this endangered those who made it, although we do know that it was not infrequent among the 'free' French workers, with whom naturally Lorenzo got along thanks to his work across the border. But it was vital to those who benefited from it. Communication was forbidden for the Jews, which gave rise to 'a deadly impression of desertion,' because 'in the great continent of freedom, freedom of communication is an important province. As is the case with health, only the person who loses it realises its true value.'[24] Indeed, 'letters meant more to prisoners than anything else: they gave a slender meaning to their lives and a sense of connection to the world they had lost',[25] as Thomson explains. It all happened in some haste, considering the circumstances. The postcard is dated 25 June and the Auschwitz postmark is from the following day. The sender is Perrone Lorenzo, Italian Group, Beotti Firm, Auschwitz ... Germany.

Primo's message, as written down by Lorenzo, reached its destination relatively quickly – in three weeks, in a context in which the letters of Italians often took several months. For two days it lay on the doormat at No. 15 Via Montebello, Turin, the home of Levi's dear friend Bianca Guidetti Serra, who, not being Jewish, was less at risk. When she saw the postcard, Bianca, unaware of the 'enormity' of what was happening in Auschwitz, felt only 'great relief'[26] at knowing that Primo was alive. For his part, Levi would admit to Thomson that he had been 'irresponsible': 'I had no idea how dangerous it was to send letters home.'[27] In so doing, he had above all compromised the safety of his Italian 'accomplice', as he himself narrated in the story 'The Juggler'.

By pure chance, another friend of the group, Primo's cousin Ada Della Torre, was staying at the time with

Levi's mother, Ester Luzzati, known as Rina. Having had a premonition, she went to Turin and telephoned Bianca, whose maid said to her: 'Come quickly!' That's how the postcard reached the hands of Levi's family.

In those first days of the second half of July, Levi's mother replied, and the letter went off, taking the inverse route. At the same time, almost 1,400 kilometres away, her son was trying to teach his disciple – Bandi, 'the diminutive of Endre ... Szántó, a name which is pronounced more or less like *santo* in Italian'[28] – the art of organisation, although the Hungarian newcomer seemed not to want to submit to the centrifugal morality of the camp.

'August came, with an extraordinary gift for me: a letter from home – an unprecedented event,' Levi would recall. His mother signed herself 'Signora Lanza', and like Levi experienced that moment illuminated by the presence of two 'saints', the one who had made it possible and the one who bore lightly the name that evoked him:

> The letter from the sweet world burned in my pocket; I knew that it was elementary prudence to keep silent, and yet I had to talk about it.
>
> At that time we were cleaning cisterns. I went down into my cistern and Bandi was with me. By the weak gleam of the light bulb, I read the miraculous letter, hastily translating it into German. Bandi listened attentively. Certainly he could not understand much because the message was scant and reticent. But he understood what was essential for him to understand: that that piece of paper in my hands, which had reached me in such a precarious way and which I would destroy before nightfall, represented a breach, a small gap in the

black universe that closed tightly around us, and through that breach hope could pass. At least I believe that Bandi, even though he was a Zugang, understood or sensed all this, because when I was through reading he came close to me, rummaged at length in his pocket, and finally, with loving care, pulled out a radish. He gave it to me, blushing deeply, and said with shy pride: 'I've learned. This is for you. It's the first thing I've stolen.'[29]

...

Two more postcards were sent, again written by Lorenzo and signed by him; while a parcel of food and clothes sent by Bianca from the post office in Sassi – a village in the foothills outside Turin – whose receipt is dated 9 August, crossed war-torn Europe for Auschwitz. The first postcard was written on 20 August and sent the following day: Primo said, through Lorenzo, that he was fine ('I am keeping in excellent health in fact with the good weather I feel better'), that his command of German was growing and that it was 'a great advantage for work' – in this way, his family would understand that he was working – and he tried to reassure the family, especially as communication was difficult and took a month. 'Don't worry about me and try to send me everyone's news. Take great courage and great hope. Accept my best wishes and an affectionate embrace from the one who always remembers you, your Lorenzo.'[30]

It was at this point that Bianca again tracked down Levi's mother and his sister, Anna Maria, who, as Jews, were living in hiding, and rushed to them in a euphoric mood: 'I have amazing news to give you, Primo has written!'[31] This time he did so in his own name. In her memoirs, which came out in 2009, she would situate this episode a month earlier, confusing it with the first communication that reached Primo's family. Thomson, after interviewing Bianca in 1993, reconstructed what happened in this correspondence between 21 August and September 1944:

> Levi's reply to his mother, copied out by Lorenzo Perrone in his own untutored hand and again sent to Bianca Guidetti Serra, passed the Auschwitz censors on 21 August. Bianca received the postcard six weeks later (mid-September 1944) and arranged to hand it to Levi's mother in Turin. 'I'll never forget the look on Ester's face when she realised that Primo may still be alive.' But after the elation, Ester pointed out that the message was sent a full month and a half ago, in which time anything could have happened. Consumed by anxiety for her *primogenito*, Ester would not see Primo for another thirteen months.[32]

But she would see him again, when it was all over, and also thanks to the 'rare good fortune'[33] of having been able to communicate with him. This was an extremely rare privilege. 'We survivors are not only an exiguous but also an anomalous minority: we are those who by their prevarications or abilities or good luck did not touch bottom': this is how Levi sums up the contributing factors that allowed some to get out alive. In a chapter entitled 'Communicating' in *The Drowned and the Saved*, he points out how much the inmates suffered from isolation from the world and 'failed or limited' communication. And yet 'not to suffer from it, to accept the eclipse of the word was an ominous symptom: it signalled the approach of definitive indifference.' This was why Lorenzo's contribution towards establishing contact with the outside world was as crucial as the soup he brought Primo and Alberto: 'this was one of the factors that allowed me to survive ... each of us survivors is in more than one way an exception; something that we ourselves, to exorcise the past, tend to forget.'[34]

Three factors saved the 'wretched aristocracy' in Auschwitz, 'the strongest, the smartest, the luckiest': prevarication, ability and good fortune. Levi was also built slightly and would remain skinny all his life (his small frame was another crucial factor in his salvation) but Lorenzo was Primo's good fortune. Don Lenta told Thomson many years later that 'in Lorenzo's day, the bricklayers and fishermen of Fossano went out of their way to help the weakest in the community.'[35] Here we may be getting to the heart of Lorenzo's story, which will take some time to digest. The idea of Auschwitz and its surroundings as a 'community' may appear jarring, and even monstrous, but at the same time it restores our faith in the human spirit. The contagion of evil did not affect everyone 'down there', there were those who had enough 'reason, compassion, patience, courage'[36] to fight it. Amid the greyness, something always shone: at 'the other end of the thread' you might find 'a friendly person'. And it's quite likely that, buried amid the millions of archive documents, the millions of words spoken, read and written, there are many other men and women like Lorenzo – hundreds, perhaps – although we only know a few.

...

While other 'free' and 'volunteer' workers were executed in their hundreds across the Nazis' crumbling European fortress for organising themselves, and dozens more escaped from the places selected as part of the Italo-German accords (mainly from Heydebreck and Blechhammer, far fewer escaped from Monowitz), Lorenzo continued transporting pints of soup and sending postcards. Meanwhile, Primo and Alberto were discussing the beneficial effects of this unhoped-for protection, 'stumbling from one puddle to the other, between the black of the sky and the mud of the road. We talk and we walk. I carry the two empty bowls, Alberto the happy weight of the full *menaschka*':

> We talk about our plan to buy a second *menaschka* to rotate with the first, so as to make only one expedition a day to the remote corner of the yard where Lorenzo is now working. We speak about Lorenzo and how to reward him; later, if we return, we will of course do everything we can for him; but of what use is it to talk about that? He knows as well as us that we can hardly hope to return.[37]

I don't think Primo and Alberto ever tried to hatch escape plans with Lorenzo. In Monowitz, it was almost impossible anyway. There were some: the so-called 'Count of Auschwitz', a British soldier called Charles Coward, helped hundreds of prisoners to escape, using a remarkable ploy: Coward 'collected chocolate and cigarettes from his fellow prisoners and exchanged them with the guards for corpses that he then substituted with Jewish inmates whom he helped [in this way] to escape.'[38] Coward was in a position of absolute privilege, since prisoners of war were able to receive packages from the Red Cross. Indeed, Coward had even had the nerve to complain to the Germans (who apologised) about the terrible conditions for inmates. He was also able to count on a 'team'.

Apart from Coward, there is only one other 'certified' case of a 'Righteous Among the Nations' operating in Monowitz or in the immediate vicinity. This was the Polish peasant Józef Wrona, who lived with his mother Anna, sister Helena and brother Eugeniusz in Nowa Wieś, near Kęty. Hired for Buna, he came into contact with Jewish prisoners, two of whom, Jacob Max Trimmer (who would later be called Max Drimmer) and Mendel Scheingesicht (later Herman Shine) he helped to escape. On 21 September 1944 – at the same time as Bianca and Ester were reading Primo's reassuring words as written down by Lorenzo, and Lorenzo himself was daily transporting the *menaschka* full of soup – Wrona cut the barbed-wire fence, led Jacob Max and Mendel out of the camp and hid them in his own home, where they remained for about two months, and then – before they were likely to be discovered – managed to transfer them to a female acquaintance of his, in whose house they lived until the liberation. 'The only way the Jews could have survived' outside the Lager, the historian Jan Tomasz Gross records in his book *Golden Harvest: Events on the Periphery of the Holocaust*, 'was with the assistance of the local population.'[39] Yad Vashem would proclaim Wrona a 'Righteous Among the Nations' on 13 March 1990, and on 12 December 2006 would extend that to the members of his family. Two other prisoners, probably both German, subsequently managed to use the gap opened by Józef in the barbed wire to escape. Nor was Wrona the only Polish worker to help the inmates. Within Monowitz, 'a desperate, hidden and continuous struggle' for survival continued, a 'continuous war of everyone against everyone', that of the 'sealed-off monads' in that world of slaves.[40]

I assume it was in the month of October – Lorenzo was now forty – that a nasty blow fell, as Levi recounts in *Moments of Reprieve*. 'Evidently somebody must have watched and followed me because one day in the hiding place I found neither mess tin nor soup. Alberto and I were humiliated by this affront and also terrified because the mess tin belonged to Lorenzo and his name was scratched on it. The thief could denounce us or, more probably, blackmail us.'[41] And here are more words of Lorenzo's – as usual, not many – which, although reported in indirect speech, give us another fragment of him:

> Lorenzo, to whom I immediately reported the theft, said he didn't care about the mess tin, he would get another one, but I knew this wasn't true: it was his army mess tin, he had carried it with him in all his travels.[42]

CHAPTER 8

The Night That Refuses to End

For more than two years and eight months, Lorenzo stood firm on the margins of Hell. We have no way of knowing if he had planned to escape – about 500 workers escaped in the first months of 1944 alone – before he met Prisoner 174,517. Nor is there any way of knowing, at a distance of decades and considering how much of the human spirit remains unfathomable, why he stayed.

Was it out of fear? Because he cared about work 'well done' and was reasonably well paid? Because he was used to roaming across the borders drawn on maps? Because he didn't have strong enough ties in Italy – especially no wife – to get home to? Because he was helping these two bourgeois in dire need? Or a combination of all these things.

What we know for certain is that he had a friend in 'Suiss' – apart from Primo. There was another man present in that lunar, bomb-ravaged landscape where Lorenzo met Prisoner 174,517: 'Peruch', assuming this was his real surname – we don't know his first name. For a long time, being familiar with Levi's habit of inserting elements of fiction into his narrative and renaming quite a few of his 'characters', I didn't investigate Peruch at all, especially as Levi himself depicted him more as a character of legend rather than of history:

> Peruch was from Friuli, and he was to Lorenzo what Sancho Panza was to Don Quixote. Lorenzo moved with the natural dignity of the person who is oblivious of danger, whereas Peruch, small and sturdy, was restless and nervous, and incessantly turned his head this way and that, with little jerks. Peruch was walleyed; his eyes diverged greatly, almost as if in his permanent anxiety he was striving to look ahead and to both sides at the same time, like a chameleon.[1]

Apart from his Friulan origins and a physical description that verges on caricature, we know nothing else about Peruch. Levi only wrote about him in the story 'Lorenzo's Return' and nowhere else as far as I know. The one concrete element that he adds in those pages is an observation that situates him halfway between Lorenzo's unconditional help and the way that some alleviated other people's hunger to avoid their hungry looks, out of either a fleeting humane impulse or morbid curiosity. Peruch helped, but did not do so systematically because he was terrified:

> He too had brought bread to the Italian prisoners, but secretly and without regularity, because he was too afraid of the incomprehensible and sinister world into which he had been flung. He would hold out the food and immediately hurry off, without even waiting for a thank you.[2]

Rather late in the day, I decided to review the millions of documents in the Arolsen Archives. How many Peruchs had left traces of themselves? Quite a few, in fact, and by a process of elimination, two attracted my attention. The first, Ettore, was born in 1908 in the Friulan municipality of Chions but could not have been in Auschwitz after March 1944 according to the German documents. The second was named Antonio, and he too was from Friuli – from Caneva, near Pordenone, if I decipher the handwritten papers correctly. He was practically the same age as Lorenzo (he was born on 22 April 1906) and worked for Colombo (owned by Mario Colombo of Rome), which is one of the firms that signed the contract simultaneously with Beotti in 1943. But it seems that he was a prisoner in Dachau by the beginning of 1945, which would clash with the information in our possession thanks to Levi, and my many telephone calls to those I assume to be Peruch's descendants led nowhere. Peruch remains little more than a shadow: there is nothing really to hold onto, since there are no lists of Italian civilian workers in the Auschwitz archives, and the documentation about them is very sparse. This shows us how difficult it is to grope our way through the millions of names of workers – slaves, forced and compulsory, 'volunteers' and 'free' – who filled the Third Reich in those years and rescue them one by one from oblivion. In many cases it's close to impossible.

...

At various times, Levi admitted his own (relative) powerlessness as a man of letters faced with the three-dimensional power of reality, starting with the most intimate aspect, the psychological. In *Auschwitz, città tranquilla*, which appeared in *La Stampa* in March 1984, he confessed that he had read dozens of books on the psychology of the oppressors and found them unsatisfactory, adding that 'this is a basic shortcoming in works of non-fiction; it almost never possesses the power to give us the depths of a human being: for this purpose, the dramatist or the poet are more appropriate than the historian or the psychologist.' Not to mention the relationship between language and action: 'the trade of clothing facts in words is bound by its very nature to fail,'[3] he would write at the end of 'Carbon', the last of the 'stories of militant chemistry' in *The Periodic Table*; 'it is impossible to transform a person into a character, that is, fashion an objective undistorted biography of him,'[4] he would reaffirm ten years later in *Other People's Trades*. A glaring example is the story 'Iron', centred on Sandro Delmastro (whom he makes the son a bricklayer in this literary transposition, although in reality he wasn't). A friend from the time of his chemistry studies and a companion on his excursions, during a period when mountaineering had become for Levi a synonym of freedom and a training ground, Delmastro could be described as one of his mentors: 'Perhaps, in some obscure way, we felt the need to prepare ourselves for future events,'[5] Levi would say, referring to the many climbs they did together. With Sandro, he learnt to survive despite the exertion, the stress, the danger, the cold, the hunger: essential 'training' at a time when, of course, he could not foresee the Lager.

In the course of one of these excursions, recounted in 'Iron', the climbers put themselves in a relatively difficult situation because, according to Sandro, 'what was the point of being twenty if you couldn't permit yourself the luxury of taking the wrong route?' In response to his friend's anxieties about getting back, Delmastro had replied, 'as for getting down, we shall see', adding mysteriously, 'the worst that can happen is to have to taste bear meat.'[6]

'Well, we tasted bear meat in the course of that night, which seemed very, very long,' Levi wrote. 'And now that many years have passed, I regret that I ate so little of it, for nothing has had, even distantly, the taste of that meat, which is the taste of being strong and free, free also to make mistakes and be the master of one's destiny.'[7] These were years in which 'slowly, confusedly, the idea was making headway in us that we were alone, that we had no allies we could count on, neither on earth nor in heaven, that we would have to find in ourselves the strength to resist,'[8] as he recalled in the story, 'Potassium'. Grateful to Sandro Delmastro 'for having led me consciously into trouble, on that trip and other undertakings which were only apparently foolish, and I am certain that they helped me later on.'[9] When recounting his friend's tragic death, he admitted the limitations encountered by trying to bring a man of action back to life. Delmastro, fighting in his local resistance group, was killed in April 1944, 'with a tommy gun burst in the back of the neck by a monstrous child executioner, one of those wretched murderers of fifteen whom Mussolini's Republic of Salò recruited in the reformatories,' Levi wrote. And here are his words on the relationship between reality and fiction, on writing as a more or less voluntary 'alteration', at the very least within the parameters traced by each of his 'characters':

> Today I know that it is a hopeless task to try to dress a man in words, make him live again on the printed page, especially a man like Sandro. He was not the sort of person you can tell stories about, nor to whom one erects monuments – he who laughed at all monuments, he lived completely in his deeds, and when they were over nothing of him remains – nothing but words, precisely.[10]

It is not a question of memory, which Levi treated with great caution and skill. He would even claim in the last part of his life, when talking about his time in Monowitz – of which he maintained that he had 'pathologically precise memories'[11] – that 'strangely, with the passing of the years, those memories do not fade or scatter, rather, they become enhanced with details I thought I had forgotten, and which sometimes acquire meaning in the light of other people's memories, letters I receive or books I read.'[12] And yet, as we read in 'Cesare's Last Adventure', the story that precedes 'Lorenzo's Return' in *Moments of Reprieve*, 'over long distances human memory is an erratic instrument, especially if it is not reinforced by material mementoes and is instead spiced by the desire [...] that the story be a good one.'[13] This is how Levi wrote about the act of bringing Lorenzo to life in *Moments of Reprieve*:

> I have also told about Lorenzo elsewhere, but in terms that were deliberately vague. Lorenzo was still alive when I wrote *If This Is A Man*, and the task of transforming a living person into a character ties the hand of the writers. This happens because such a task, even when it is undertaken with the best intentions and deals with a respected and loved person, verges on the violation of privacy and is never painless for the subject. Each of us, knowingly or not, creates an image of himself but inevitably it is different from that, or, rather, from those (which again are different from one another) that are created by whoever comes into contact with us. Finding oneself portrayed in a book with features that are not those we attribute to ourselves is traumatic, as if the mirror of a sudden returned to us the image of

somebody else: an image possibly nobler than ours, but not ours. For this reason, and for other more obvious reasons, it is a good practice not to write biographies of the living, unless the author openly chooses one of two opposed paths: hagiography or the polemical pamphlet, which diverge from reality and are not impartial. What the 'true' image of each of us may be in the end is a meaningless question.[14]

Levi's caution here is evident, coming as it does after a number of incautious 'transformations'. I'm thinking of Piero/Cesare, the 'cunning and ingenuous' character in *The Truce* in whom the man who inspired Levi – Lello Perugia – would not have recognised himself, and of Endre Szántó, the 'disciple' in the story of the same name, who Levi hoped would 'find himself' in the pages devoted to him. And Sandro Delmastro's family would not have appreciated Levi's portrait of him.

...

It was around October 1944 that Alberto found the man who had stolen Lorenzo's mess tin. He then had the idea of offering Elias three rations of bread, in instalments, so that the latter should recover 'by fair means or foul' that object so dear to Lorenzo. In 'Lorenzo's Return', Levi would say that the latter accepted because 'he liked to show off', that he confronted the thief – a Pole like him – and that, after fighting for ten minutes, he gained possession of the mess tin. 'From then on he became our friend,' Levi comments, and Lorenzo got his tin back.

It was also in October 1944 that the cold arrived. The pages that describe the advancing nightmare are among the most heartrending of *If This Is A Man*: anyone who has read it and re-read it feels the cold throbbing in his eardrums from time to time. This was a cold that has no connection with what a free human being feels, a murderous cold, greeted in the most unbearable silence.

> We know what it means because we were here last winter; and the others will soon learn ... we will have to keep our muscles continually tensed, dance from foot to foot, beat our arms under our shoulders against the cold. We will have to spend bread to acquire gloves, and lose hours of sleep to repair them when they become unstitched. As it will no longer be possible to eat in the open, we will have to eat our meals in the hut, on our feet, everyone will be assigned an area of floor as large as a hand, as it is forbidden to rest against the bunks. Wounds will open on everyone's hands, and to be given a bandage will mean waiting every evening for hours on one's feet in the snow and wind.
> In the same way in which one sees a hope end, winter arrived this morning. We realised it when we left the hut to go and wash: there were no stars, the dark cold air had the smell of snow. In roll-call square, in the grey of dawn, when we assembled for work, no one spoke. When we saw the first flakes of snow, we thought that if at the same time last year they had told us that we would have seen another winter in Lager, we would have gone and touched the electric wire-fence; and that even now we would go if we were logical, were it not for this last senseless crazy residue of unavoidable hope.[15]

Seven out of ten prisoners would die.

But in Auschwitz and the other extermination camps, where hope and the family were allies of the murderers – and bearing in mind that induced suicide remains a de facto homicide – suicide was not as common as we might imagine. The commitment to cling to life – or else, alternatively and conversely, to sink – was too strong.

...

Two things happened in that extraordinary time that further reversed the order of that world outside the world.

The first was a true miracle: a package arrived from Italy. As Levi recounts in 'Last Christmas of the War' it had been sent by his sister Anna Maria and his mother Rina, hidden in Italy, 'through a chain of friends … the last link of that chain was Lorenzo Perrone.' The package contained ersatz chocolate, cookies and powdered milk, but Levi describes its 'real value' to him and Alberto as 'beyond the powers of ordinary language.' It was an 'unexpected, improbable, impossible package' 'like a meteorite, a heavenly object, charged with symbols, immensely precious, and with an enormous momentum.' The weight of this package was not due so much to the contents as to 'a link with the outside world.'[16]

Almost half the precious gift was immediately stolen, but the rest helped to keep the two of them alive. 'We divided up the contents of Alberto's pockets. His had remained unscathed, and he proceeded to display his finest philosophical resources. We two had each more than half the food, right? And the rest wasn't completely wasted. Some other famished man was celebrating Christmas at our expense, maybe even blessing us. And anyway, we could be sure of one thing: that this would be our last Christmas of war and imprisonment.'[17]

THE NIGHT THAT REFUSES TO END

The existence of this miraculous delivery is revealed in the third and last postcard written and sent by Lorenzo on 1 November 1944, and which reached its destination, in which he speaks in the plural:

> 1.11.44.
>
> Carissima Abbiamo finalmente ricevuto quanto da tempo attendevo poi immaginare che gioia la salute si mantiene buona malgrado i primi freddi e il morale stabile ti prego di informare la famiglia dellavolta di brescia ti prego sempre sempre ti sogno notti intiere di te e la nostra casa e la nostra [...] come era e speriamo sarà [...] Dio voglia che ci possiamo ritrovarci presto ti prego ti far tanto che puoi perche io o tanta fiduccia in te. e ricevi un cordiale saluto da chi sempre ti ricorda tuo affessianatissimo.
>
> Lorenzo. addio ciau

The third of Primo Levi's letters sent by Lorenzo Perrone, 1 November 1944.

> Dear friend we finally received what I was long waiting for imagine what joy we're keeping well despite the first cold weather and our morale is firm please inform the Della Volta family in Brescia always always I dream whole nights of you and our house and our life as it was and we hope will be again please God we will meet again soon please keep going because I have a lot of confidence in you receive this heartfelt greeting from one who always remembers you yours very affectionately.
>
> Lorenzo goodbye ciao

The second astonishing episode concerns Lorenzo directly. I mentioned it early in this book, and it's one of those cases – of which there are not so many in Lorenzo's life story – where we can contrast what Levi wrote close to the event with what he wrote thirty-five years later. In *If This Is A Man*, the indirect account of a dialogue between Primo and Alberto reads: 'we ought to do something at once; we could try to have his shoes repaired at the cobbler's shop in our Lager, where repairs are free (it seems a paradox, but officially everything was free in the extermination camps). Alberto will try: he is a friend of the head-cobbler, perhaps a few pints of soup will be enough.'[18] In this account, the outcome is not revealed. Only in *Moments of Reprieve*, half a lifetime later, would Levi linger on what happened in the last days of 1944, immediately after Lorenzo's firm refusal to give Primo his sister's address:

> However, in order not to humiliate us by this refusal, he accepted from us another form of compensation, more appropriate to the place. His leather work boots were worn out; there was no shoemaker in his camp, and

repairs were very expensive in the city of Auschwitz. But in our camp anyone who had leather shoes could have them repaired free, because (officially) none of us were allowed to have money. So one day he and I exchanged shoes. For four days he walked and worked in my wooden shoes, and I had his repaired by the Monowitz shoemakers, who in the meantime had given me a pair of temporary replacements.[19]

We have to imagine those days when Lorenzo found himself literally in someone else's shoes, or rather, a tightrope walk in mismatched clogs, which had given Primo ulcers the scars of which would remain for the rest of his life. It was during this window of time when Levi realised that he could make it out of there.

In this story in which people walked close to the ground, where life and death depended on shoes, soup, postcards sent and a package received, Levi had the brazen good fortune during the days of glacial cold to be chosen – and not for the gas chamber. After months of rumours that the polymerisation laboratory housed in Building (*Bau*) 939 needed professionals, and after an actual 'exam' taken on 21 or 22 July, Levi was chosen to work there. He entered the laboratory and the smell made him 'start back as if from the blow of a whip.'[20] Stawinoga, a young German Pole in charge of the laboratory, who assigned workplaces to him and the other recruited slaves, tried to avoid talking to them but called them 'Monsieur', which Levi found 'ridiculous and disconcerting'. The Russians were just eighty kilometres from the camp. Buna was in ruins and enveloped in a tomblike silence. The French civilian workers were walking upright and the British prisoners of war made the victory sign to the *Häftlinge,* indicating that the end was near. This is the context in which Levi ended up indoors, where he would presumably not be beaten and where there would be 'fabulous new things to steal. If he weren't such an old camp hand by now, he might even begin to hope.'[21]

The final 'fortune' for Levi, a few days later, was to fall ill with scarlet fever (which Alberto had had as a child). This happened at the perfect time. Had it happened earlier, being considered expendable, it would have led to Levi's death. Had it happened any later, Levi would already have been on the death march. He fell ill 'just once, but at the right time', he told Philip Roth. The unhoped-for admission to the laboratory at the end of 1944 was crucial. The other slave labourers were hastily evacuated, among them, Primo's old friend Franco Sacerdoti. And it was in those first weeks in the warmth that the final encounter in the camp between Primo and Lorenzo took place, on the threshold of the 'House of the Dead', but both still alive.

...

When speaking of Lorenzo, Levi always took care to say that wondering about a person's 'true' image is 'a meaningless question'. But it can't be denied that there are times when Lorenzo seems to take on the role of a natural counterbalance to the petty and mean-spirited acts of many others 'down there' – and of each of us. Even though 'perfection belongs to narrated events, not to those we live,'[22] Lorenzo comes close to it.

It could be objected that Lorenzo exists only as a literary character who appears in Levi's works in a fragmentary fashion. This is partly true. But we should also take into account public occasions when Levi spoke about Lorenzo.

One such is the conversation with Professor Alvin Rosenfeld in Indiana, in the presence of the latter's students, in April 1986, in which Levi would remember Lorenzo as a man of Catholic culture but an unbeliever, 'very simple, uneducated': 'he really was someone out of the ordinary' driven 'by an irrepressible urge to help [...] for purely moral reasons.' 'He could barely write,' Levi would add, 'but he felt obliged, morally, to help people who needed help.'

Considering the fragmentary nature of the documentation that we have, it's hard to relate this rounded-out character to the real person. That real person was usually silent and moved with his head bowed, but he kept his eyes open and was diligent, attentive and compassionate. He was a real misfit, that much is clear, because he refused to submit to the sinister logic of that upside-down world, not even when he would have been entitled to do so. Perhaps he was ill-suited to life in general, given those actions of his that gave the lie to a world in which prevarication was the rule. This is shown, if proof were still needed, by the two men's last encounter 'down there', which happened around 26 December 1944, when there was another American air raid on the I.G. Farben plant:

> At the end of December, a short time before I fell ill with that scarlet fever which saved my life, Lorenzo had started working near us again and I could again accept the mess tin directly from his hands. I saw him arrive one morning, wrapped in a short, gray-green military cape, surrounded by snow, in the work grounds devastated by the nighttime bombings. He walked with his long, assured, slow step. He handed me the mess tin, which was bent out of shape and dented, and said that the soup was a bit dirty.[23]

Inside the mess tin there were 'pebbles and grit'. When Primo asked Lorenzo to explain, Lorenzo 'shook his head and left'. It wasn't until a year later that Levi discovered that 'Lorenzo's camp had been hit that morning by an air raid. A bomb had fallen close to him and had exploded, burying the mess tin. It had also burst one of Lorenzo's eardrums, but he had come to deliver the soup anyway.'[24] Five years later, Primo reported that Lorenzo had ended up along with the soup 'in the bomb crater', and the earth shifted by the explosion had spattered into the bowl and perforated his eardrum; 'he was half deaf that day', but he didn't tell Primo, he kept it to himself. For an interview, he shared Lorenzo's exact words, in Piedmont dialect. 'I'm sorry, *ah l'è 'n po' sporca eh la zuppa.*' ('The soup got a bit dirty.') A few hours or days later, together with Peruch, Lorenzo left.

CHAPTER 9

Walking

It was like a moving river in full spate. From January 1945, for at least three seasons; 'men passed by on foot, often barefoot, with their shoes hanging from their shoulders to save the soles, because the march was long; with or without uniforms, armed or unarmed, some singing lustily, others grey-faced and exhausted.'[1] This is how Levi remembers his days in Staryje Doroghi in *The Truce*, published in 1963. He spent two summer months in 1945 in limbo, having escaped the slaughter, witnessed the arrival of the Soviets and begun his geographically illogical and literarily picaresque wanderings.

Lorenzo was already a long way away. He had notched up a good many of the interminable kilometres that would take him back to Piedmont: 1,412. I doubt he put his hat on before leaving (I don't even know if he had one 'down there') but he'd almost certainly done everything he could to hold on to his grey-green cape. He no longer had his patched-up sweater, a 'rag of clothing' in Angier's words, which he had given to Primo to wear under his *Häftling* uniform, although we have no idea when.

The final payment to Lorenzo was made on 15 January 1945 by the firm Colombo, indicating that Lorenzo had changed employers in the final phase of his stay in 'Suiss', although still in the context of the infamous Italo-German accords. He may have left before he was authorised to do so. It could have been an actual escape, or at least a slightly premature departure. Lorenzo had definitely left Camp Leonhard Haag along with all the other male workers by 21 January 1945, six days before the arrival of the Red Army and following the 'Lothar' evacuation order the previous day. According to Levi's account in 'Lorenzo's Return', Lorenzo left Monowitz in a mad rush because he 'knew that the Russians were about to arrive, but he was afraid of them. Perhaps he was right: if he had waited for them, he would have returned to Italy much later, as in fact happened to us.'[2] And so early in January 1945, having only 'a very vague idea of the geographical position of Auschwitz,' Lorenzo set off with Peruch:

> The two men left on foot. From the Auschwitz station they had taken a railroad map, one of those schematic and distorted maps on which only the stations are indicated, joined by the straight lines of the tracks. They walked by night, aiming themselves toward the Brenner, piloting by their map and the stars. They slept in haylofts and ate potatoes they stole in the fields; when they were tired of walking they stopped in villages where there was always work for two masons. They rested by working and requested payment in money or kind. For four months they walked.[3]

We can think of him recharging his batteries in one of the many abandoned places discovered on the way or camping out in grass-strewn courtyards, bivouacking just like 'thousands of foreigners [...] in transit like us, belonging to all the nations of Europe.'[4] It is quite unlikely that Lorenzo was one of those 'who had worked (voluntarily or not) in the German factories'[5] situated in Rawicz, a town to the north-west of Auschwitz. On the basis of the documentation in our possession we can deduce that his itinerary, heading south-west and passing through Czech territory then Austrian territory, was from the start decidedly more linear. Even too linear, from what Levi would say in his dialogue with Rosenfeld, venturing the hypothesis that Lorenzo was afraid of the Russians 'perhaps because he was influenced by Nazi propaganda.'

> The two men walked for four months, by night, taking their bearings from the stars, hiding during the day in order not to be recaptured by the Germans. They oriented themselves in an odd way. They stole a map in a station. But you know what those maps are like. They have straight lines between one map and the next. They're not suitable for the normal process of finding your bearings. That's why they walked for such a long time, because they constantly misread the map, and because they had to stop during the day to rest and look for food.[6]

The documentation collected by Levi's biographer Angier is irreplaceable. It's not in the Yad Vashem file but in her archives, which are now kept at the Primo Levi International Study Centre in Turin. It was amazing to be able to put together the pieces of the puzzle thanks to these new acquisitions, just as I was writing the second half of this story. Apart from confirming certain things I hadn't been able to confirm from the selection of sources Angier submitted to Yad Vashem – such as the fact by January 1945, Lorenzo had been working for Colombo for several months, his final payment from Beotti dating from 9 May 1944 – this documentation, although fragmentary in nature, allows us to trace crucial details. For example, that at least once between December 1942 and the beginning of 1943 Lorenzo went home, returning to Germany between 27 and 29 January; also that he was paid in an irregular manner (sometimes weekly, sometimes monthly), in the two full years he spent 'down there', working as a bricklayer at 0.76 marks an hour – although Angier is careful, like Levi and like Bermani, to put quotation marks around the 'voluntary' nature of his job.

Another thing we learn, thanks to the employment record here reproduced in full, is that in March 1942, on his way to Auschwitz, Lorenzo passed through Tarvisio, but his position is indicated as one of *bétonnier*. The fact that the word is in French whereas all his other particulars are in Italian suggests that Levi may have been right: perhaps Beotti did recruit him and others in France. The mystery is not solved by the sparse documentation unearthed by the Chamber of Commerce, after many requests and months of waiting, nor are there any trace of ads by Beotti in the local newspaper *La Fedeltà* of 18 and 25 March.

In any case, given that he was at the central police station in Cuneo on 30 March and 14 April and that on 16 April in Treviso he was issued a visa to 'go to Germany through the pass from Tarvisio' within three days, it is beyond question that he crossed over from French territory. As for his homecoming, Angier managed to partly reconstruct the journey of Lorenzo and Peruch, summarising it in this way: 'at the end of April they were in Bruck-an-der-Mur in Austria, where they were given exit visas to leave the Reich via Arnoldstein, near Villach.'[7] The documentation she based this on shows that Lorenzo was actually in Bruck-an-der-Mur from 28 April to 10 May 1945. Assuming that they had departed between 1 and 15 January, the date of the last payslip, the journey lasted five months, not four.

Perhaps 'cheating' slightly, Levi situated the crossing of the border not at the pass near Tarvisio, where it in fact happened, but 250 kilometres further west – at the Brenner, which he himself crossed on the way there, in February 1944, and on the way back, in October 1945 – and gives it the date of 25 April, when Northern Italy rose up and Anglo-Americans and Soviets shook hands in a Berlin in flames. Between the end of April and the beginning of May, Lorenzo had a narrow escape on the Italian border, when they came under fire from a tank of the escaping German forces. By the second half of May, when his friend Primo was still pursuing his labyrinthine itinerary across Central and Eastern Europe (Belarus, Ukraine, Romania, Hungary, Czechoslovakia, Austria, Germany, then Austria again), Lorenzo was definitely back in Italy.

...

'If we return, we will of course do everything we can for him; but of what use is it to talk about that? He knows as well as us that we can hardly hope to return.'[8] This was what Primo and Alberto thought and said to each other. At the time when Lorenzo started out on his legendary walk from Buna with Peruch, there were 9,792 prisoners alive in Monowitz, 9,054 of whom were Jews.

About 1,670 had died in the previous years, not including the systematic 'selections' that had sent the weakest or those considered unfit for work to the gas chambers in Birkenau – a camp Levi never saw as a prisoner and which, he would recall, killed 24,000 people in a single day, in August 1944. Setkiewicz's calculations, based on the work of many decades and an impressive accumulation of data, have made it possible to enumerate the many thousands of prisoners sent to the gas chambers. The total number of victims at Monowitz may rise as high as about 10,000, and that is a conservative estimate that reveals only part of the horror relating to the I.G. Farben factories.

To give a vague idea of the desolation the survivors left behind them, on the day Lorenzo arrived – 17 April 1942 – more than 1,000 deportees had reached Auschwitz, and fifty had died; on the day he left, 100 Polish men and 100 Polish women were shot in Crematorium V at Birkenau; and as he took his first steps alongside the railway tracks, there were 11,493 women and girls in the same Lager, as well as 202 children, according to the official camp documents. Broadening our field of vision to the whole history of 'Planet Auschwitz', in four years and eight months 1,100,000 people were murdered, ninety per cent of them Jews. The 'lucky' ones, the one in four who survived selection on arrival and the devastating impact of the Lager, had worked as slave labour before dying. Thanks to the scarlet fever he had contracted, Levi remained in the camp hospital, together with 800 other inmates. The others, including Alberto Dalla Volta, left. 'He saluted Primo awkwardly – "Arrivederci, buona fortuna" – and walked out to his likely death.'[9] Alberto was among the drowned, a monad lost in that 'grey army of ants'[10] that was dragged across the landscape of an almost defeated Third Reich, after sharing bread one last time with Primo 'in the trust and friendship that united us':

Alberto left on foot with the majority of the prisoners when the front drew near: the Germans made them walk for days and nights in the snow and freezing cold, slaughtering all those who could not go on: then they loaded them on open freight cars, which transported the few survivors to a new chapter of slavery, Buchenwald and Mauthausen. Not more than a fourth of those who left survived the march.[11]

...

The only letter we know of that Primo sent to Italy during his return journey, a page and a half handwritten in pencil and addressed to Bianca Guidetti Serra, is dated 6 June 1945 and was posted in Katowice. 'I am alive by a miracle,' he wrote, saying how he had been saved by the scarlet fever and probably by luck, because there was no time to murder him and the others who had remained in the hospital. 'Then, on 27 January, the Russians arrived.' From what is described as a 'holding' camp, Levi makes the grim observation that of those who had left Fossoli with him just over a year earlier, only five were still alive. After saying that Vanda Maestro had certainly died, he adds that 'of the ninety-five of us in the Monowi[t]z camp, seventy-five died there of starvation or disease'; fourteen were deported by the fleeing Germans, and as to their fate, including that of Alberto, 'worrying rumours are circulating'. Of the 650 who left Fossoli in February 1944 and who were reduced to ninety-six, ninety-five, ninety-four, ninety-three, and so on, three would return together. The total number of survivors was twenty-four. 'Don't believe what I was able to write from Monowi[t]z,' he insisted, as if there were really any need – the number tattooed on his left arm would remain a 'document of infamy not for us, but for those who are now starting to atone.' And in a long P.S. he adds, among other things:

> I am dressed like a tramp, I may well arrive home without shoes, but in return I've learnt German and a little Russian and Polish, and I've also learnt how to get by in all kinds of circumstances, how not to be discouraged, and how to withstand moral and physical suffering. I have a beard again, to save money on barbers. I can make cabbage and turnip soup and cook potatoes in all kinds of ways, all without condiments. I can assemble, light and clean stoves. I've practised an incredible number of trades: assistant bricklayer, labourer, garbage collector, porter, gravedigger, interpreter, cyclist, tailor, thief, nurse, receiver of stolen goods, stonecutter: even chemist! I was forgetting: I've lost touch with the wonderful Lorenzo Perrone, but it's likely he's safe: did you track down his sister? I think she lives in Turin, at 15 Via San Francesco da Paola (or d'Assisi). Nobody knows how much I owe that man: I'll never be able to repay my debt.

The man to whom Levi owed much more than just a small part of his salvation is described in the heat of the moment as nothing less than 'wonderful Lorenzo', because he had not merely given him support that was concrete, untiring, heedless of the risks, rooted in down-to-earth action. This was not a story that could be summed up in a few lines, as Levi would soon do in *If This Is A Man*:

> In concrete terms it amounts to little: an Italian civilian worker brought me a piece of bread and the remainder

of his ration every day for six months; he gave me a vest of his, full of patches; he wrote a postcard on my behalf to Italy and brought me the reply. For all this he neither asked nor accepted any reward, because he was good and simple.[12]

No, it hadn't been only the soup, the sweater, the postcards. It was hope.

> However little sense there may be in trying to specify why I, rather than thousands of others, managed to survive the test, I believe that it was really due to Lorenzo that I am alive today; and not so much for his material aid, as for his having constantly reminded me by his presence, by his natural and plain manner of being good, that there still existed a just world outside our own, something and someone still pure and whole, not corrupt, not savage, extraneous to hatred and terror; something difficult to define, a remote possibility of good, but for which it was worth surviving.[13]

Was it possible to repay his debt?

Lorenzo, having entered a refugee camp on 19 May, probably reached Turin two weeks later, at the beginning of June, at the same time as Levi's letter to Bianca left Katowice. The shadow of war still hung over the city. The first days of the month had seen a peak in the number of killings; there were Fascist snipers at work, and there was much settling of accounts, some of it private.

What did Lorenzo look like at this time? Apart from the two black and white photographs we have already seen, the first from twenty years earlier, the second presumably from this period, we have a few extra details at our disposal. Angier's archives actually give us a physical description from 30 March 1942, a few days before he left for the Third Reich, when his passport was issued. A 'pinkish' complexion, brown eyes and brown hair – in other words, immediately before 'Suiss' there was not yet a clear trace of grey. It's surprising to discover that Lorenzo was one metre seventy-one centimetres tall: not a negligeable height for the time, but certainly not as tall as I would have expected for a 'giant'. I have decided to reveal this here, since the data is confirmed by his earlier military records, with the addition of a few details: at that time his eyes were described as grey, and his chest measurement was eighty-five centimetres.

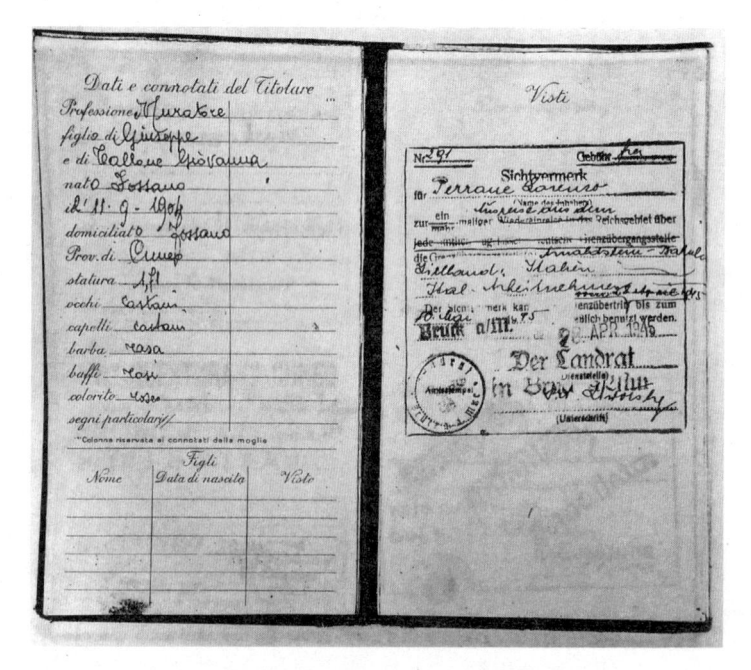

Lorenzo Perrone's passport, 30 March 1942.

While Lorenzo might not have been a giant, his size clearly conveyed this impression to all those who met him, particularly to Levi, who was 'small, skinny'[14] and always among the smallest in the various photographs of him and in the memories of his fellow prisoners. But three years after crossing the border at Tarvisio and heading for Poland, the image of Lorenzo had changed. According to the many testimonies we have, he weighed a maximum of forty kilograms by the time he reached Italy. Now that he was over forty, his hair had turned grey, and his appearance must have been off-putting. But he was not ill: the certificate that he received from the refugee camp has no mention of hospitalisations or health problems, nor does he seem to have received clothes before his return.

He was certainly not the only person to cross Europe towards Italy in this state during those months. He was one of the many returning from the 'German inferno', a 'tide of starving tramps', as Lazzero Ricciotti puts it in his book *Gli schiavi di Hitler*.[15] 'They come back on foot, or clinging to trains and lorries, they proceed in short stages, they beg, they sleep as they can, they march like sleepwalkers towards the Brenner, towards Tarvisio, towards the seven thousand Italian municipalities,' we read in an article in *L'Epoca* on 23 May 1945. 'Including soldiers and workers, there are about a million men.' Accustomed to crossing to France clandestinely, this time Lorenzo had travelled quite legally: his passport, renewed twice in Wroclaw, was valid until 24 May 1945. When he reached Turin, Lorenzo tracked down Primo's family, and was unable to lie:

> After the Brenner, Peruch was almost home and headed east. Lorenzo continued, still on foot, and in about twenty

days arrived in Turin. He had my family's address and found my mother, to whom he brought news of me. He was a man who did not know how to lie; or perhaps he thought that lying was futile, ridiculous, after having seen the abomination of Auschwitz and the dissolution of Europe. He told my mother I would not return, that the Jews in Auschwitz were all dead, from the gas chamber, or from work, or killed in the end by the fleeing Germans (which was almost literally true). Moreover, he had heard from my comrades that at the Camp's evacuation I was sick. It was best for my mother to resign herself.[16]

Later reconstructions confirm the episode as narrated by Levi, with some negligible discrepancies and with a few extra details: he was 'shy and awkward'[17] in addressing Ester, according to Thomson – who places this sequence of events a few days earlier – and these were Lorenzo's words as Levi would report them to Rosenfeld: 'Yes, I saw him, I helped him, I gave him bread and food, but he's ill, I don't think he'll make it back.' He was a 'ragged, cadaverous man, so patently honest and hurt', and he gave Levi's mother 'his dreadful message in a voice he rarely used': this must have shaken Rina, Angier writes. But she 'did not show it', rather, 'she sat him down at the table and prepared a meal for him, with many glasses of wine.'[18] Then she offered him money to take the train home. But he – of course – refused. 'He had walked for four months and who knows how many thousands of kilometres; there really was no point in getting on a train,'[19] Levi wrote in 'Lorenzo's Return'.

He took the last sixty kilometres on foot: twelve hours' walk but first, he went to see Primo's sister Anna Maria at the headquarters of the National Liberation Committee in Via Maria Vittoria. He was 'unbelievably wretched' and 'so inhibited by my presence that he could scarcely speak,' she told Thomson on 19 October 1992.[20] Levi said later to Rosenfeld: 'He was so simple, he couldn't conceive that sometimes it was best to tell a white lie.'

At last, Lorenzo set off for home. In Genola – scene of a terrible massacre on 28 April 1945 – he met an old friend, Cino Sordo, riding on a cart. He was now a mere hour and a half away from his house in Via Michelini. Cino – whom Levi remembers incorrectly as a cousin of Lorenzo's – offered to give him a lift, 'but at this point it would have really been a pity, and Lorenzo arrived home on foot, come the way he had always travelled all his life.'[21] 'To him time meant little.'[22] Anyway, Cino rushed to Fossano to tell everyone that Lorenzo was alive, in very bad shape, yes, but alive. 'Tacca' was back.

At about the same time, Primo, was regaining his strength more than 1,000 kilometres away. He was also experiencing a complicated relationship with time. He was living a lethargic life in exile, his work and suffering having abruptly stopped. In that limbo he 'perceived the heavy breath of a collective dream,' of that point in which 'nothing acts as a screen between a man and himself; perhaps because we saw the impotence and nullity of our life and of life itself, and the hunch-backed crooked profiles of the monsters generated by the sleep of reason.'[23] Lorenzo too had known the hunch-backed crooked profiles of those monsters. And after so much horror, the world was straightening up again, leaving behind what had to remain behind. In the year 1945, the 'sledge-dogs',[24] such as Levi had been, gradually returned to an upright position, while Lorenzo continued to walk with head bowed. Everything was back in its place. More or less.

PART IV

What will you say, what will I say, if we shall also find ourselves ... Walking westward? Will we be able to rejoice in the name of the species, and of those others who within themselves find the strength to reverse their course?

— Primo Levi, 'Westward'

CHAPTER 10

Us Few Still Alive

We shouldn't imagine that a bricklayer returning alive after three years away on foot after walking more than 1,000 kilometres, in the year 1945, should be greeted by a brass band or hold his head high. His homecoming was announced by his friend Cino, who I imagine was quite struck by Lorenzo's physical appearance. A hulk of a man reduced to forty kilograms, perhaps even less according to what his relatives told Angier, must have made quite an impression. So much for the Fascist propaganda that had portrayed the 'volunteer' workers as well rewarded and well fed! For a man of Lorenzo's size, his weight was now almost half what it should have been, less than Levi had weighed at the age of fifteen. Lorenzo also had a noticeable scar on his thigh when he got home. Apparently in Monowitz, his friend Primo had also managed to source some medicines for Lorenzo to prevent infection following a nasty cut on barbed wire.

Apart from these few crucial documentary fragments that have made it possible to retrace the journey in broad terms – the memories of Primo's mother and sister and the fleeting encounter with Cino in Genola – we know nothing of Lorenzo's five-month odyssey. But now, probably in the first half of June 1945, he had almost arrived home as it was in the post-war period. Living in the house – the numbering of which had changed, now covering both No. 4 and No. 6 of

Michelini – there was Lorenzo's father Giuseppe, his mother Giovanna and his little niece Emma, who was about to turn eight. I don't know if on the day Cino met him in Genola, his three brothers – Giovanni, Michele and Secondo – and his sister Caterina were there. Giovanna was definitely in Turin. In any case, when Cino rushed to Giuseppe, the latter 'took his mule and cart to Genola to bring his son home.'[1]

But Lorenzo, who had stopped at the house of another friend just outside Genola, once again rejected the lift. 'He would walk, and in his own time,'[2] reports Angier. I can almost see him, sending his father away with an irritable gesture and a few muttered syllables in Piedmont dialect. *Gaute*, go away, father. I'll be there, *un moment*. Giuseppe also mainly expressed himself mainly in non-verbal language, and so he did at that point. Angier again:

> Perhaps Giuseppe did not want to tell his wife that their son would not come home; or perhaps he didn't speak because he never spoke, and it was too late to change. Or perhaps the story is a family myth: dramatised, half-imaged, but such a powerful image that it is immediately believed. This is what it says: Lorenzo finally re-entered via Michelini 4, emaciated, grey, his shoes in tatters and his feet covered in sores. He put his sack down on the floor, and it was crawling with lice. His young niece Emma stared at him, terrified. Giovanna, his mother, said sharply, 'Chi e Lei? Cosa vuole?': Who are you? What do you want? 'Mamma,' he said. 'I'm Lorenzo.' Since this is a Perone story, it does not tell if Giovanna cried. It says only that she handed him a few things from his sack, among them the dented mess tin; and took the rest and burned it.[3]

'*Còsa vol chiel?*' ('What does this one want?') were the exact words that Grandma Giovanna uttered, as her granddaughter Emma, whom I meet seventy-seven years later, remembers it.

'*But Mama, son Lurenz*' ('I'm Lorenzo'), he replied.

...

The tattered shoes, the sores, the fleas, the jute sack. It was time to make a clean sweep: everything had to be thrown away, although Lorenzo held onto the mess tin. Perhaps because it held that beautiful memory – it seems incredible, but he still had beautiful memories, as we shall see – of when Primo and Alberto lost it and then, thanks to Elias, got it back for their friend Lorenzo. Now that peace had come; human life was starting to hold a certain value again, not at all like 'down there'.

The critical threshold was high in general, and in the Granda in particular, in the spring of 1945. At a time when Lorenzo and Peruch had still not reached the Austro-Italian border, the health authorities in the Cuneo region had recommended 'the decontamination of people and clothes' for those who had returned from Germany to avoid the spread of infectious diseases. All over Europe, hygiene offices had been working ceaselessly for months. As fragile peace became a reality, it was still necessary to be aware of possible outbreaks and epidemics.

In Fossano, work had resumed in factories and shops had reopened early in May, on the orders of the Resistance high command. By the end of June, the mayor decreed that all those displaced by the war must immediately return to their own municipalities. At the beginning of July, the weekly *La Fedeltà* wrote that 'day by day we have the joy of welcoming the return of some of our fellow citizens from Germany,' trusting that the numbers would increase. Returnees were entitled to a 'bonus' of 5,000 lire 'and a length of material for clothes' – apart from those who 'went to Germany voluntarily', whose 'political conduct' and 'financial situation' would need to be investigated. 'Most of the survivors from Germany', the National Liberation Committee wrote at the end of the month to a health official, 'are in a deplorable state of health and require extra nutrition', and in its final report would recall how 'deeply preoccupied' those now in charge were 'with the problems inherent in feeding the public' and the 'distress of the less affluent classes'. In the file of the Fossano branch of the National Liberation Committee, kept in the city archives, which includes investigations into the records of a large number of citizens, there is no trace, among the thousands of papers containing requests, declarations, denunciations and interrogations, of any welfare payments requested and obtained by Lorenzo. The possibility that he did apply cannot be ruled out, nor that he may have been unaware of the opportunity – but, having gained a rough idea of his character over the years, I do not think that he would have easily allowed anyone to investigate his 'political conduct' or 'financial situation'. Nor is there any trace of his receiving material help from the 'great' Charity Bank held on Sunday 16 September 1945: neither his name nor his signature figure among the hundreds of receipts still preserved. On a list of representatives of various categories of workers attached to the documentation of the Fossano branch of the National Liberation Committee about this charity initiative, which had been announced on 28 August, the name of his brother Giovanni appears, written by hand, with the description 'seasonal bricklayer'. From this I deduce that the Committee had made a request for Giovanni to be helped with 'food and clothing' or else through 'offers of money'. Lorenzo's legendary pride might well have been amplified by this: in a circumscribed place like the *Burgué*, a brother who asked for help could have given rise to lies and gossip, and it cannot be ruled out that at least part of the community considered him a collaborator because of his having worked for the Germans. Sheltered behind the four walls of Via Michelini, Lorenzo was holding on to his hunger and his few rags.

Material problems, however stifling, were merely one side of the coin, and in some respects the more reassuring side, because they were tangible. Italy was emerging from twenty years of dictatorship, five years of conflict in Europe, and twenty months of civil war on home soil. While celebrating the thirty-eight citizens of Fossano who fell in the Resistance, the (Catholic) periodical *La Fedeltà* invited its readers to rid themselves of the previous years' poisonous hatred. 'For five long years we have breathed hatred,' an article said, admonishing even those who had rebelled. 'Something of it has remained in our lungs. These are harmful germs that have invaded our organism, and of which we need to free ourselves as soon as possible.' Nothing could have been truer, if applied to Lorenzo.

'Il Tacca' was not only emaciated, filthy and wounded, but his change was beyond physical. He hardly ate, he dressed any old how, and his silence was particularly stubborn and impenetrable. It would have been difficult to communicate what he had seen. Very little was known of the crimes that had been committed – images of the horrors of the camps had not yet been widely disseminated and even the local press were quite confused. Those places where people had been killed through work, like Dachau and Mauthausen, and the extermination camps that had been part of the 'final solution', were far away.

Many years later, in 1992, Lorenzo's youngest brother, Secondo, aware of the horror contained in that name which at the time was exotic – Auschwitz – told Thomson: 'when I asked Lorenzo where the hell he'd been, he refused to say and lurched off with a drinking crony. He didn't want to talk about Auschwitz, what he'd seen there, to anyone.'[4] At about the same time, Mayor Manfredi, having talked to both Secondo and Lorenzo's other brother Michele, the tinsmith who would become the municipal plumber responsible for fountains, wrote in a local newspaper that Lorenzo 'never talked about what had happened to him in Germany [sic].' 'Lorenzo would never have told his family what he had done in Auschwitz,'[5] Angier, the person who has done the most to probe the memories of his relatives, says in her biography of Levi. 'However solitary and difficult he had been before, he was much more so afterwards,' she wrote in 1997 to Yad Vashem's Mordecai Paldiel, pursuing the procedure to have him officially declared 'Righteous Among the Nations'. He had come home, yes, but not truly. On one of those first days at home, Lorenzo 'was found half-dead from brandy and fatigue in a field.'[6]

The first documented event of significance at which Lorenzo was present was the death of his father, a few days after they met in Genola. On Tuesday 3 July 1945, that brutal, violent man, who had probably never hugged his children, considering it something to be ashamed of, breathed his last. Lorenzo didn't go to register the death: it was his two younger brothers, the thirty-three-year-old Michele – who signed himself Perone with one 'r'

– with the thirty-two-year-old Secondo who did so. They declared that their father Giuseppe, seventy-eight, a scrap merchant, had died at 9.30 in the morning. The weekly *La Fedeltà* reported the news a few days later, as it did regularly with birth and deaths. What remains an absolute mystery is the fact that the two brothers declared their father the 'widower of Giovanna Tallone', when in fact their mother would live another eight years. (Why didn't they read what they wrote? Because they and the registrar didn't understand each other?) It would be undeserved speculation to suggest that Lorenzo didn't go to register the death because he resented his 'old man'. It may be more honest to admit that, despite everything, he might actually have been quite attached to his father. But I don't think that's the point. Quite simply, I don't consider it plausible that Lorenzo was relieved at this death. Yes, he might have experienced it as an ironic coincidence, because his relationship with abuse of power, with prevarication, with violence – even justified violence, I would hazard – had been radically transformed.

Looking back at those years begun amid the brawls at the 'Pigher' or some other place, and the repetition of automatic behaviour passed down from generation to generation, what is most evident is that, after 'Suiss', all this seemed to have vanished. The fact remains – if we may speak of 'fact' since we can trust only to family memory – that in one way he had changed, and the immediate death of his father may have helped him in that direction. That atavistic violence that had accompanied him from his birth, the violence of those at the bottom of the ladder, the blows taken and given, the fights, the sticks and knives, that anger that had lasted centuries and generations, had gone away with his father. Lorenzo was still a man of few words, he was a sad man, a very sad man, perhaps already a desperate man, prone to alcoholism and self-destruction, but he no longer had the ability to harm other people.

...

'The Lorenzo Perone episode is perhaps the highest point of Primo Levi's testimony,' Angier wrote to Lorenzo's niece Emma in 1995, forty years after he had returned home. 'Primo Levi made the story of Lorenzo Perone a centrepiece of his investigation of Man.' It is not an insignificant statement, coming as it does from one of the people who not only knows Levi's visible profile but who has done the most work to investigate his intimate self. It is a striking thing, picking up the Italian and English editions of the Angier and Thomson biographies (both of which are told chronologically), to realise that Levi was not yet halfway through his life in 1945 – he was twenty-seven, and would live for another four decades – that, confronted with a man who was already old at the age of forty, Primo had basically intuited everything there was to understand. Levi's inquiry into human nature, which is the private meaning of his work, starts with *If This Is A Man*.

Let me put it like this: if Levi had seen in Lorenzo something halfway between a brother and an adoptive uncle (in his family, 'uncle' was an elastic term: two of Levi's uncles on his mother's side were practically the same age as Lorenzo, born like him at the beginning of the century), for Lorenzo, who was fifteen years older, it may be that his friend, the young Turinese, was more like the son he hadn't had. Cesare Levi, Primo's father, who was over forty when he was born, had been an absent and distant father who loved to 'distinguish [himself] from the vulgar crowd'[7] and had died during the war (24 March 1942), when Lorenzo was about to cross the border at Tarvisio and Primo had not yet made his decision to join the Resistance. During the one period when Levi had 'lived' far from his home in Turin (apart from a brief interlude in Milan in 1942–3), Lorenzo had taken care of him as only a father could.

When Levi reached home, one of his first thoughts was to find Lorenzo. He revealed in an interview how, in the days after Auschwitz was liberated, 'suddenly your neighbour was no longer your adversary in the struggle for life but a human being who was entitled to be helped.'[8] The final pages of *If This Is A Man* tells how he reacquired a sense of humanity together with two French fellow prisoners, Charles Conreau and Arthur Ducarne, helping the sick and the dying and recovering a sense of pity, which previously 'one couldn't act on,' which 'was dispelled almost on conception'[9] when you were hungry. Lorenzo, although on the margins, would never lose that sensitivity, and Primo knew that when he reached home on 19 October 1945.

The final scene of his 'truce' would remain imprinted on the memory of those closest to Levi. Bianca Guidetti Serra rushed with other friends to Levi's home as soon as she heard the news, where he was with his mother Rina and his sister Anna Maria. They shook hands and said 'Ciao': at that time, and in that social milieu, people didn't hug. 'I don't think I ever hugged Primo,' she would admit with a laugh in a French documentary. It's possible Levi was never hugged even by his mother. Levi thanked Bianca for helping Rina 'and for taking Lorenzo's letters to her,'[10] and rediscovered 'the liberating joy of recounting.'[11] 'He had found his task for the rest of his life.'[12]

Levi had a long beard, he was in rags and bloated, as

described at the end of *The Truce* – he had eaten potatoes for six months. He would recall (also laughing, almost relieved) in another television programme in the presence of his sister Anna Maria that he was unrecognisable to many. In those first weeks, his deep-rooted shyness disappeared and he began to talk to everyone: he was becoming a storyteller. He had always been a great listener: 'I am one of those people to whom many things are told,' he wrote in *The Periodic Table*, adding, 'and I'm definitely not complaining about it.'[13] The Alsatian Jew Jean Samuel, No. 176,817 in Monowitz, who had lived in the same hut as Primo and Alberto, would maintain on several occasions that Primo had the great quality of getting people to talk, listening and remembering. About the 'art of listening',[14] Levi would say, many years after his return, 'I am a man who speaks and listens, I am very struck by other people's language.' And at the same time: 'It's very important to understand each other. Between the man who makes himself understood and the man who doesn't make himself understood there is a profound difference: one gets saved, the other doesn't. Was one of his aims, now, to get Lorenzo to talk? They would now spend a reasonable amount of time together.

Three or four months after Lorenzo's homecoming and a few weeks at most after his own, perhaps at the end of October, and definitely by 3 November 1945, Levi went to Fossano. It was a time when 'the sensitivity and willingness to help others' were, perhaps, at their highest. A Day of Solidarity was announced by the Christian Democrats and supported by the other parties to encourage offers of money, clothes, foodstuffs and 'anything that can alleviate the misery, suffering, struggles and anxieties of so many wretched and destitute families.' The Fossano municipal assistance authority distributed 150 kilograms of wool yarn at a controlled price to families considered to be unquestionably in need. This is how Angier summarises what she had learnt from Lorenzo's family:

> Now this is a Levi story as well as a Perone one; but neither, of course, describes the moment of meeting. The Perones say only that *il Dottor Levi* brought a knitted vest for Lorenzo, to thank him for the one Lorenzo had given him in the Lager. It was white, with a red border at the neck, and made of goat's wool; Lorenzo kept it until he died, but (they exchange a smile) it was so rough and scratchy that he may never have worn it.[15]

The episode of the vest is key, considering what had just happened: it's no coincidence that Angier's archive, in which we find notes of her interviews, and her letters to Lorenzo's relatives, reveals a kind of contagious obsession with the details of this vest. It was of goat's wool, had a red border at the neck, and was white; perhaps a counterbalance to the greyness that had hung over their parallel and intertwined lives 'down there' in Monowitz. A white sweater for the winter: the perfect turnaround for a man who had been floundering and in dire need and who now holds out his hand to his saviour, and in that hand an emblematic, simple, powerful gift. It may have been just a simple white vest, warm but uncomfortable, but I find it moving and logical that Lorenzo kept it until the day he died, even though he probably never wore it. As Samuele Saleri puts it so well in his unpublished thesis:

A gesture of gratitude, almost a symbol that will superimpose itself on the patched-up jacket that had allowed the prisoner to protect himself from the cold. A sweater for the winter, all in one piece, handed over by a free man to a free man. Now the two can be friends, they can see each other without obligations or prohibitions, they can talk to each other and ask each other, 'How are you?'

...

As hugging was clearly not practiced, did they shake hands, the first time they met on the outside? Did the thin hands of the chemist and the rough hands of the bricklayer bring about that friendship, or did they keep a re-established distance? Lorenzo's were brown according to his passport, grey according to his military papers; Levi's blue. How did Lorenzo and Primo look at each other, watched by the Fossano community, which surely could not have failed to notice, and to gossip about, this anomaly of the friendship?

Immediately after seeing Lorenzo, Primo published a text which may be the very first piece of his to appear in print (with the exception of a negligible poem from his schooldays). It appeared in a magazine on 22 June 1946, but would bear the date '28 December 1945', which is presumably correct. This is certainly the first time he wrote about Auschwitz with a public in mind, and it is a poem. The literary scholar Sophie Nezri-Dufour revealed on the occasion of the centenary of Levi's birth in 2019 that *The Truce* was also originally conceived as a poem. As Levi himself declared, his first impulse as a witness was to express himself in poetry, although later he wrote very few poems.

This one is called *Buna*:

> Torn feet and cursed earth,
> The long line in the grey morning.
> The Buna smokes from a thousand chimneys
> A day like every other day is in store for us.
> The whistles terrible at dawn:
> 'You multitudes with dead faces,
> On the monotonous horror of the mud
> Another day of suffering is born.'
> Tired companion I see you in my heart.
> I read your eyes sad friend.
> In your breast you carry cold, hunger, nothing
> You have broken what's left of the courage within you.
> Colourless one, you were a strong man,
> A woman walked at your side.
> Empty companion who no longer has a name,
> Forsaken man who can no longer weep,
> So poor you no longer grieve,
> So tired you no longer fear.
> Quenched once-strong man.
> If we were to meet again
> Up there in the world, sweet beneath the sun,
> With what kind of face would we confront each other?[16]

It may be a case of auto-suggestion – this poem speaks above all to the many who were drowned, and certainly not to the 'free' workers – but it's hard not to glimpse traces of Lorenzo in these lines. They had already met again by the time it was written, and perhaps that meeting made Levi aware of the absence of the all too many who had vanished 'down there'. Beyond that, I do see something of Lorenzo in it: the 'tired companion' with 'torn feet' whom Levi sees 'in my heart', the 'quenched' man who once was strong, and that final question: 'If we were to meet again / Up there in the world, sweet beneath the sun, / With what kind of face would we confront each other?'

The two of them, the 'volunteer' worker and the slave labourer, the slave chemist, were given that opportunity to meet, and many times. And in that 'sweet world' they had regained, the two men looked each other in the face: one who was sinking, the other who was catching a glimpse of the light of that 'sun' – although Levi would take many months to 'lose the habit of walking with my glance fixed to the ground, as if searching for something to eat or to pocket hastily or to sell for bread.'[17] And they shook hands: Lorenzo's was certainly rough, Primo's noble but neglected, a future 'faithful collaborator of the brain', as he put it. A few weeks later, Levi started to write in prose, and he would never stop, beginning what Belpoliti defines as his 'adventure as a storyteller and speaker'. The two things were intertwined: the books of testimony were born out of the stories, and *If This Is A Man* was born 'backwards', developing out of the many words uttered by a young man finding his voice at the end of 1945.

The so-called *Auschwitz Report* which Levi wrote with a fellow prisoner, the surgeon Leonardo De Benedetti, 'a good man' who would later appear as a character in *The Truce*, saw the light of day in the July-December 1946 issue of *Minerva medica*, the most important medical journal of the time. It was a kind of 'factual' matrix of the masterpiece *If This Is A Man*. Between the writing and the publication of the report, *If This Is A Man* was completed – not spontaneously, but in a well thought-out manner. During this time, Levi also shared these memories of Lorenzo, in *Moments of Reprieve*:

When I too had gotten back, five months later, after my long tour through Russia, I went to Fossano to see him again and bring him a woollen sweater for the winter. I found a tired man; not tired from the walk, mortally tired, a weariness without remedy. We went to the *osteria* for some wine together and from the few words I managed to wrest from him I understood that his margin of love for life had thinned, almost disappeared. He had stopped working as a mason. He went from farm to farm with a small cart buying and selling scrap iron. He wanted no more rules or bosses or schedules. The little he earned he spent at the tavern; he did not drink as a vice but to get away from the world. He had seen the world, he didn't like it, he felt it was going to ruin. To live no longer interested him. I thought he needed a change of environment and found him a mason's job in Turin, but Lorenzo refused it. By now he lived like a nomad, sleeping wherever he happened to be, even in the open during the harsh winter of '45–'46. He drank but was lucid; he was not a believer, didn't know much about the Gospel, but he then told me something which in Auschwitz I hadn't suspected.[18]

This is the only testimony written by Levi about what happened to Lorenzo after the summer of 1945. Other fragments of this narrative come from various interviews and documentation. To Caracciolo, Levi would tell it this way, his eyes watering:

He would say, 'there's no point living in a world like this.' He'd been a bricklayer, he was a good bricklayer, but he'd stopped working as a bricklayer, he bought and sold scrap metal, and whatever money he made went on drink: and when I went to see him every now and again in Fossano I'd ask him, 'why are you living like this?' and he'd say quite coldly, 'there's no point living, I drink because I'd rather be drunk than sober.'

To Rosenfeld:

Once he'd returned home, he didn't resume his work as a bricklayer, because he was a wounded man. Not physically; he was wounded morally. The things he'd seen in Auschwitz, the same things that leave so many people indifferent today, had wounded him. And he'd lost the will to go on living. He started drinking. I tried in vain to dissuade him, but he told me, very coldly, 'why should I go on living in this world?' Because of the drink he started walking unsteadily, in winter he'd fall in the snow. He fell drunk in the snow several times.

...

The way Levi would tell the story in 'Lorenzo's Return', as far as we can discover by crosschecking it with other sources, corresponds almost entirely to the truth. There is no trace of a work contract between 1945 and 1946, and according to all those who remember, Lorenzo worked as a scrap merchant, a *feramiù*, like his father. He displayed his merchandise on Wednesdays near the entrance of the Iride cinema, according to Don Lenta, who had researched the matter 'among a few elderly inhabitants of Fossano who had been businessmen or bricklayers in the Borgo Vecchio before the war.' All his siblings and relatives interviewed in the 1990s by Thomson and Angier confirmed that Lorenzo had stopped working, and so would the local researchers, guardians of the community's memory. And yet for a few weeks at least he must have kept himself busy, as evidenced in a remarkable discovery of Angier's in the archives. In a brief letter to Emma Dalla Volta (mother of the 'inseparable' Alberto) dated 3 November 1945, Lorenzo recounts what happened to him, probably in September: 'Fell while collecting firewood and hurt myself so badly and had to stay a month in hospital and now I'm out and limping the things that happen in life.' But he definitely worked mainly as a scrap merchant: that much is certain.

Michele Tavella, born in 1940, who has collected dozens of photographs of the *Burgué* and its inhabitants throughout the twentieth century, has shown me one from those years of a scrap merchant pulling his two-wheeled cart, his hat pulled down over his forehead, while two little girls behind him smile at the camera. The man is sitting, and we can't see his face, but I'm pretty sure it isn't Lorenzo. As implied in another story by Levi, 'The Guerrino Valley', it cannot be ruled out that Lorenzo would occasionally fall asleep on his cart. He was confused, exhausted, desperate.

Do we understand from Levi's accounts that Lorenzo did indeed verbalise his situation to his friend? Here, a final interview between Levi and Motola offers an unprecedented and surprising mention of the atmosphere of the Cold War:

> He asked me once, very laconically, 'Why are we in the world if not to help each other?' Full stop. Period. But he was afraid of the world. Having seen people die like flies at Auschwitz, he wasn't happy anymore. He was not

a Jew, not a prisoner himself. But he was very sensitive. After he returned home, he took to drinking. I went to him – he lived not far from Turin – to persuade him to stop drinking. He'd abandoned his job as a bricklayer and used to buy and sell scrap iron because he was an alcoholic. He drank every lira he earned. I asked him why, and he told me outspokenly, 'I don't like living any more. I'm fed up with life ... After seeing this threat of the atom bomb ... I think I've seen everything ...' He'd understood many things, but he didn't even realise where he'd been. Instead of *Auschwitz*, he used to say *Au-Schwiss*, like Switzerland. He was confused in his geography. He couldn't follow a timetable. He'd get drunk and sleep in the snow, completely drunk with wine.

Lorenzo was despondent now, because he was no use to anyone. This would be expressed clearly in a letter to Yad Vashem by Carole Angier, perhaps the person who knew Lorenzo best even though she had never met him. As she put it, he let himself go 'not just because he had seen too much evil, but because he could no longer do good.' As Levi put it, 'in "Suiss" Lorenzo had been a rich man, at least compared to us, and had been able to help us, but now it was over; he had no more opportunities.'[19] He was 'afraid of the world', he had lost interest in living; he hadn't 'even asked to be born'. And at the same time as everything starts to break down, he lost the desire to build.

...

A few traces of the time Primo and Lorenzo spent together exist. Among the memories of those family members who were then adult but are no longer around for me to question, there is one in Thomson's Levi biography that I find disturbing. Lorenzo's brother Secondo recalls that the first time Primo visited, 'morosely, Perrone evaded the subject of Auschwitz and, with a drunkard's truculence, told Levi to go away.'[20] Thomson sums up the 'homecoming' like this:

> Once, he had been a youthful, broad-chested athlete in Italy's crack Bersagliere army corps; now he was a drinker, and Levi could smell it too, the cheap grape brandy on his breath. Perrone spent his last lire on brandy and he had taken to sleeping off his hangovers in hedgerows and icy ditches. Levi managed to find him a bricklayer's job in Turin, but his old profession was hateful to him now. All Perrone could look forward to was the village festival of St Anna (26 July) when there was forgetfulness and free drink.[21]

He did work in Turin, at least for a few days. Lorenzo's niece Emma, who had moved to the city to attend elementary school, and who was very attached to Uncle Lorenzo, recalls that she and her mother went to meet him at the station, at Porta Nuova. But I assume the encounters between him and Levi took place mostly in Fossano. There is another faint trace of this time, an unpublished one, which I found among Angier's amazing papers, preserved partly in Italian and partly in English. According to Secondo, Lorenzo's brother, Primo Levi called their mother 'Mamma'.

...

What did Lorenzo and Primo talk about?

It's hard not to think of the images we find in Levi's works. In *The Wrench*, above all, where Faussone — let's not forget that, by Levi's own admission, this was his alter ego – who does nothing but talk, after a while, 'contrary to his habit', breaks off and walks 'silently at my side, his hands behind his back, his eyes fixed on the ground'. It's almost as if Lorenzo is suddenly there.

The glimpses we are given a few years later in *If Not Now, When?* are impressive if we want to gain an idea of the hours they spent together. Of two characters, Levi writes that 'they would be silent for a long time, savouring that relaxed and natural silence born from reciprocal trust: when you share deep experiences you don't feel any need to talk.'[22] Another of Levi's alter egos, the watchmaker Mendel, and his double, Leonid, about whom I've already written, comparing him specifically to Lorenzo (although Leonid was not a great drinker, and nor for that matter was Mendel), allow us entry to these moments of which the only trace is a few mumbled sentences. Leonid, who has just been talking about his unfortunate family history, concludes: 'and now I've had enough. Enough walking towards God knows where. Enough of blood and frogs, and I want to stop, and I want to die.' The narrator writes at this point:

> Mendel didn't answer; he realised his companion wasn't one of those men who can be healed with words; perhaps nobody with a story like his behind him could be healed with words. And yet Mendel felt in his debt: guilty towards him, at fault, as if he were seeing a man drown in shallow water and, since the man doesn't call for help, allowing him to drown. To help Leonid you had to understand him, and to understand him, he would have to talk, and he talked only like this: a few words, then silence, his eyes avoiding Mendel's.[23]

And much further on, after an unhinged and inconclusive 'flight' and just before his death caused by a suicidal act, it is said of Leonid, this 'good boy with a nasty temper', that 'his suffering began much earlier than ours', and that 'he would be a man to be treated'. It's hard to believe that Levi did not transfer many of those silences and those words, at the 'Pigher' and in the *Burgué*, into this character, in those very years when he spoke and wrote quite often about Lorenzo. And it's likely this also influenced the construction of the character of Mendel, driven by a 'dumb need for decency' and who now and again fantasised about being seized by 'weariness, emptiness, and a yearning for a white, serene nothingness, like a winter snowfall.'[24]

When the winter of 1945 arrived, 1,412 kilometres from where Lorenzo had left Primo a jumper, they were back in their rightful place. As far as we know, they often – perhaps very often – arranged to meet at the 'Pigher', where Lorenzo apparently had a table reserved, or they went together to Via Michelini. How were they dressed? In the case of Lorenzo, we already have an idea; as for Levi, I imagine him as he is portrayed in Antonio Martorello's play about Lorenzo, *Io vi comando*, which was performed twice in Fossano in March 2022: elegant, as was common at the time, especially for a chemist at the beginning of his career, with polished shoes. But he was lost, out of place. Even though Levi loved surrounding himself with common people – 'factory hands, wine producers, metalworkers,'[25] Thomson would write – it's hard to imagine him sitting amid the tables in the 'Pigher' gulping litres of wine.

The 'Pigher' was so called because of the owner's nickname. Tavella tells me he would say to his wife, without lifting a finger, 'Bring the *mês s'tup*' ('the half bottle of wine'), hence the dialect nickname *pìgher*: in Italian, *pigro*: lazy.[26] In Fossano, as in other places, such nicknames replace the real surnames ('Tacca', another example), a habit still common in the *Burgué*. At the 'Pigher', people would argue, play cards – especially *tresette* – sing to guitar accompaniment, and drink dark wine. The place was a dump, but held good company.

At the time of the encounters between Lorenzo and Primo, even the priest Francesco Bertotti, then in his sixties, if he wanted to meet men and women 'of the people' he had to catch them at the 'Pigher' and sit down with them. 'Come on, prior, have a drink with us,' those whose souls he wanted to save would say to *don Bêrtôtt*. Here he is in a description by the bard of the Fossano community, Mayor Manfredi: the place where 'bricklayers and fishermen with ready tongues and salacious jokes represented the people, blunt, rough, indifferent to power and the proprieties; and where life was wretched and heard-earned; this was the kingdom of Don Bertotti, the prior who knew the misery and the grandeur of his flock [...] it was a world without taboos, the world of the smiling women who went down to the Rocheis to beat their washing on the hard stone ...'[27] At the 'Pigher', people sang, played music and shouted, smoothing over, at least a little, the harsh reality; as illustrated by a photograph published by Manfedi, dating from a few years later, showing the place packed with 'bricklayers, labourers, fishermen, rough and ready people who might well punch each other in the face but then are bigger friends than before: all it takes is a glass of wine.'[28]

We have no way of knowing how much strait-laced Primo Levi drank. In *The Search for Roots*, imagining an impossible encounter with the eighteenth-century poet Giuseppe

Parini, he describes how we would have liked to have spent some time with him, 'perhaps at table, in the evening, beside a lake, drinking vintage wine in moderation.'[29] He also describes alcohol as the 'essence, the *usìa* [...] which gladdens the spirit and warms the heart.'[30] From experience he knew that wine 'loses the bite of alcohol' when you're at a great height: 'it eliminates fatigue, loosens and warms the limbs, and leads to a fanciful mood,'[31] as he wrote in 'Bear Meat'. Even in the camp, Levi managed to get drunk on methanol, according to an article he wrote for *La Stampa* a year before he died. He also knew the sensation of having 'had a lot to drink' of a 'nasty, murky wine,'[32] a sensation described brilliantly in *The Wrench*:

> Wine has never agreed with me. That wine, in particular, plunged me into an unpleasant condition of humiliation and impotence. I had not lost lucidity, but I felt my ability to stand up gradually weakening, and thus I feared the moment when I would have to rise from the bench. I could feel my tongue growing thicker, and my visual field, especially, had irritatingly narrowed, and I witnessed the unfolding of the two banks of the river as if through a diaphragm, or rather as if my eyes were peering into a pair of those tiny opera glasses they used in the last century.[33]

Taking Faussone in *The Wrench* as his transfigured and distorted alter ego, we can imagine that there were times, at least, speaking of Lorenzo, when alcohol 'hadn't clouded his mind, but had somehow stripped him, had broken through his armour of reserve. I had never seen him so taciturn, but, strangely, his silence created more closeness than distance.

He drained another glass without greed or appreciation, rather with the bitter stubbornness of someone swallowing a medicine.'[34] Of Sante, a character in the story 'Guests', in which it appears that Levi wanted to put the best of himself or of human beings in general, he observes that 'it had been a while since he had last gone calmly to the tavern: because going in, knocking back a drink and running away is like not even going there at all.' And indeed Lorenzo's drinking seemed more 'a metabolic necessity, like water on the plains'[35] than anything else. Levi certainly knew the effects of alcohol (he even had a favourite whisky, Ballantine's), and thanks primarily to his legendary spirit of observation, was good at describing them. The Soviet captain in *The Truce*, Ivan Antonovich Egorov, 'blind drunk, fitted up with an enormous pair of trousers which reached to his armpits, while his tails swept the floor,' is described as 'overcome by a desperate alcoholic despondency' and spoke 'in a sepulchral voice, amid resounding sobs and fits of tears'.[36]

What language did they speak in during these encounters? Levi understood Piedmontese dialect, 'it's my language, the language of my childhood, which my father used with my mother and my mother used with the tradespeople', he recalled. He spoke it quite well, I believe, but was perfectly clear about the difference between this language and Italian (or French, English and German): dialect is 'an essentially spoken language'.

> He spoke Piedmontese, which immediately made me ill at ease: it is not good manners to reply in Italian to someone who speaks in dialect, it puts you immediately on the other side of a barrier, on the side of the *aristos*, the respectable folk, the 'Luigini,' as they were called by

my illustrious namesake; but my Piedmontese, correct in form and sound, is so smooth and enervated, so polite and languid, that it does not seem very authentic. Instead of a genuine atavism it seems the fruit of diligent study, burning the midnight oil over a grammar and dictionary.[37]

In the 'Pigher', masks fall: the smooth, elegant, polite man opposite Lorenzo, rough but genuine. The Levi who was always among the top of his class, who studied chemistry to try to give order to chaos, who walked and climbed, but from choice rather than necessity, who had never known how to fight back, not even in self-defence, but instead took the blows 'not out of evangelic saintliness or intellectual aristocracy, but due to intrinsic incapacity,'[38] was now, after the parenthesis of Auschwitz, sitting in the tavern. Facing him was a man who hadn't advanced beyond his third year of school, who by the age of ten had already started to work and who, when Primo was sitting in a laboratory and climbing mountains at weekends, walked for weeks, sometimes clandestinely, spewing anger, straining every sinew in the service of one boss or another, cursing all creation. Primo Levi, who never lost his temper, even in his schooldays, one of the calmest, most discreet, most easy-going men in the world (it was a matter of self-discipline, not of innate balance: Levi was nervous, he could be stern and even ruthless, but with words) was facing 'Il Tacca'. And as we have seen, Lorenzo – surprisingly – spoke. Like Delmastro, he probably 'spoke as no one speaks, saying only the core of things.'[39] It was on these occasions that Levi memorised a lot of what we now know: for example, on one of them Lorenzo told him the background of the episode of the dirty mess tin, when he had shattered his eardrum. Perhaps 'the conversation did not take on life, it flashed for a moment and then was doused, like a fire made with damp wood;'[40] or perhaps they had discussions.

In a way, Levi was at home in Fossano. His family was originally from Bene Vagienna, just a few kilometres away. In some interviews, he would place these origins even closer: for example, in an interview from 5 May 1986, '[Lorenzo] was from Fossano and my father was from Fossano and so they even had some mutual acquaintances'. The question of their 'mutual acquaintances' had been one of their first topics of conversation, even 'down there'. Levi would mention it several times, for example to Caracciolo: 'now by a greater stroke of luck, my family has a branch in Fossano near Cuneo, we even had mutual acquaintances, and this bricklayer, whose name was Lorenzo Perrone, knew some aunts of my father's.' These aunts of his father's are almost mythical; the biggest mention is in the one text published by Levi in which the surname Perrone appears, just a few months before his death. 'A few years ago, I happened to introduce a man named Perrone to two aunts of mine who lived in the provinces. My aunts immediately translated this surname to Prùn, and throughout the conversation they continued to address him as *Munssü Prùn:* he himself took this as quite natural.' And a little further on: 'I was quite struck by this, because the phonetic distance between Perrone and Prùn is large, and because although I was local, I didn't know that *prùn* meant squirrel.'[41] The story continues with an entertaining etymological survey and a series of anecdotes about squirrels, but that's not the point. In another interview (with Giorgio Bocca), broadcast in 1985, we are again told that Levi had introduced Lorenzo to his aunts, and that these 'uncultivated, provincial, deaf old aunts' had 'immediately reconstructed Signor Perrone's real name; Perrone was a fake name, the real one was Prùn'. In the final anecdote in the story, Levi talks about coming across a little squirrel in a biochemistry lab. It was a prisoner, in a cage slowly rotating which forced it to walk constantly 'to avoid being dragged along', since 'in that laboratory they were doing experiments on the problem of sleep.'

> The squirrel was exhausted: it was scampering heavily on that endless road, reminding me of galley slaves rowing, and those other convicts in China who were forced to walk for days and days inside cages like this one to raise the water for irrigation channels. There was nobody in the lab; I switched off the motor, the cage stopped moving and the squirrel immediately fell asleep.

CHAPTER 11

From One Who Always Remembers You

It was during one of their visits when they were back home, that Lorenzo told Primo the secret that Primo had not suspected previously:

> Down there he helped not only me. He had other protégés, Italian and not, but he had thought it right not to tell me about it: we are in this world to do good, not to boast about it.[1]

Lorenzo 'Il Tacca', 'St Anthony', 'Don Quixote', *Munssü Prùn*, had few words: his hands were too busy helping. He had risked his life hundreds of times for both neighbours and distant strangers. And while his friend Primo was searching obstinately for the profound meaning of his whole existence, he himself was irreparably losing the meaning of his own.

This is a story about Lorenzo, not about Primo Levi. It isn't the story of a new life starting but of a life that was inexorably ending.

...

The firm of Beotti continued its activities after the war. At the end of the year, it transferred its head office to Via Tempio, still in Piacenza, and less than twelve months later would begin the reconstruction of a building in Via Pontaccio in

Milan. It ceased activity in 1966. It's worth going back to the contract that Beotti and Colombo signed in 1942 since, in the attachment on the various posts of the workers, the bricklayers were requested to 'be able to carry out plastering and walls, including coating with "Klinkerite"'. Lorenzo's skills were crucial in post-war Italy. Considering the severely ruined country he had come back to, he should have had no difficulty in finding work, but from his employment record issued in 1937 and covering the whole of the last phase of his life, he seems to have been unemployed for long periods. I have already mentioned that there is no trace of a contract in 1945, or in the following year, despite his mention of firewood and the memory of his niece Emma, which may refer to a relatively brief period. On the contrary, he appears to have been registered continuously with the Employment Exchange in Fossano (as had already happened once before, in July 1940, I presume when he'd had to rush back to Italy after the 'stab in the back'). All becomes clear when we remember that traditionally it was quite common for the bricklayers of Fossano to work as day labourers, and that his was a trade typically practised between the ages of sixteen and forty, rarely beyond that. At the beginning of the twentieth century, more than seven out of ten bricklayers in Fossano had been between eleven and forty-five.

Apart from selling scrap from his two-wheeled cart, it seems Lorenzo did do a little bricklaying work: in that chaotic post-war period, nobody paid too much attention to formalities. But given the number of times he was formally hired between 1942 and 1945 – by Saporiti for the airport at Levaldigi, then by Beotti and Colombo for Monowitz – this condition of chronic unemployment is striking. Even in the Lager, as Levi wrote, 'work could instead at times become a defence. It was so for the few in the Lager who were made to exercise their own trade: tailors, cobblers, carpenters, blacksmiths, bricklayers; such people, resuming their customary activity, recovered at the same time, to some extent, their human dignity. But it was also a defence for many others, an exercise of the mind, an escape from the thought of death, a way of living day by day; in any case, it is a common experience that daily cares, even though painful or irksome, help take one's mind off more serious but more distant threats.'[2] But Lorenzo didn't want to defend himself, or at least not like that: 'work well done' was clearly not enough to deceive the mind. He had never before lost his dignity, but now, he was suffering.

In the immediate aftermath of the war, 'the old fell silent, the young lived,' the librarian Menardi told Saleri. Photographs of this period confirm this. You just have to look at the young men of the *Burgué* in the 1940s, and you can almost feel their vitality in your bones.

Apprentice bricklayers learning their trade
in Fossano's old quarter, early 1950s.

Young inhabitants of Fossano's borgo, with the local priest Don Cavallo, 1943 and 1947.

Was Lorenzo, at the age of forty-one, old? In the eyes of the effervescent young men of the *Burgué* he probably was. He faded away in the time he had spent at home after 'Suiss'. Michele Tavella, who was attending elementary school at this time, remembers the family well: Giovanni (who had a respiratory problem in those years, he tells me), the tinsmiths Michele and Secondo, with whom he would later work ('He liked me a lot, that one'), and their sister Caterina. He doesn't remember Giovanna: she had left Fossano with her daughter Emma. Of Lorenzo, whom he couldn't have helped encountering in those years – he lived, and still lives, a mere twenty metres from where Lorenzo lived – Tavella has no memory. 'They say he didn't go out, that he didn't have many friends,' he tells me.[3] The fact is, while there was no lack of work for bricklayers in Fossano, Lorenzo 'almost never left the house', as confirmed by his nephew Beppe in 2020.[4]

...

Postcard sent by Lorenzo to Primo, 1946.

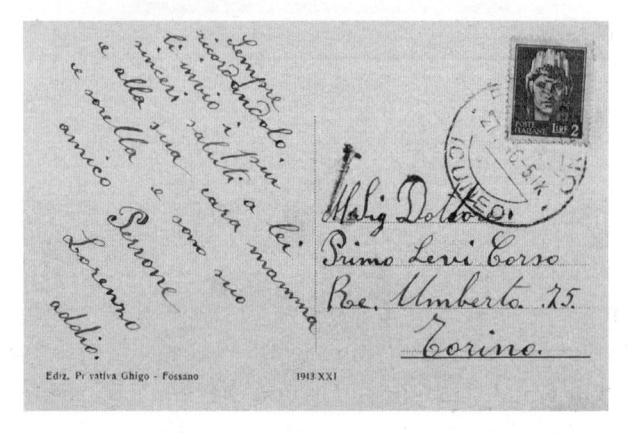

The first thing Lorenzo wrote to Primo is concise and heartrending. 'Always remembering you I send the most sincere greetings to you and your dear mamma and sister and I am your friend Perrone Lorenzo goodbye.' It's a postcard with a view of Fossano, the postmark is faded – the place is Cuneo but the date could be either 27 February or 27 July 1946, and it's addressed to 'Sig Dottore Primo Levi'.

Lorenzo addresses Primo here with the polite form 'Lei', and sometimes in other places, even with 'Voi'. Immediately on the outside, theirs was an asymmetrical relationship, like many of those that Levi cultivated: 'I am a chemist, expert in the affinities between elements, but I find myself a novice faced with the affinity between individuals; here truly all is possible, it is enough to think of certain improbable and lasting marriages, of certain one-sided and fruitful friendships,'[5] he would write in the preface to *The Search for Roots*, which was published almost simultaneously with 'Lorenzo's Return.' I knew they had written to each other, but nothing remains of the 'dozens of letters' that Primo sent Lorenzo. Angier tried to track them down in the 1990s, without success, finding only the one that Lorenzo wrote to Emma Dalla Volta, which is preserved in her archive.

But then the sensational news reached me from the Primo Levi International Study Centre on the first day of summer 2022, as if to close the winter from which they emerged. Some of these letters from 1946 still exist, they were written and kept, and they are a factual anchor for the first year of peace, at least in this segment of Europe.

And if all we have of Lorenzo for the year 1946 is these few – but wonderful – lines, Levi on the contrary was like a river in full spate. 'Talking is the best medicine,'[6] he writes in the story 'The Molecule's Defiance'. He cured himself of the Lager by the use of words. In the harsh January of 1946, 'when meat and cold were still rationed, nobody had a car, and never in Italy had people breathed so much hope and so much freedom', Levi was finding it hard to live. 'The things I had seen and suffered were burning inside of me; I felt closer to the dead than the living, and felt guilty at being a man, because men had built Auschwitz, and Auschwitz had gulped down millions of human beings, and many of my friends, and a woman who was dear to my heart.'[7] But a solution was at hand:

> It seemed to me that I would be purified if I told its story, and I felt like Coleridge's Ancient Mariner, who waylays on the street the wedding guests going to the feast, inflicting on them the story of his misfortune. I was writing concise and bloody poems, telling the story at breakneck speed, either by talking to people or by writing it down, so much so that gradually a book was later born: by writing I found peace for a while and felt myself become a man again, a person like everyone else, neither a martyr nor debased nor a saint: one of those people who form a family and look to the future rather than the past.[8]

Fate had in store for Levi 'a different and unique gift: the encounter with a woman, young and made of flesh and blood, warm against my side through our overcoats, gay in the humid mist of the avenues, patient, wise and sure as we were walking down streets still bordered with ruins.' Lucia Morpurgo became his wife in September of the following year, and thus 'in a few hours' he felt 'reborn and replete with new powers, washed clean and cured of a long sickness'.[9]

> My very writing became a different adventure ...
> Paradoxically, my baggage of atrocious memories became
> a wealth, a seed; it seemed to me that, by writing, I was
> growing like a plant.[10]

At this point the two friends went in totally different directions: one blossoms and the other fades away. Keeping faith with his promise to Alberto to do all that he could for Lorenzo, Levi tried to help Lorenzo with money and clothes, but it seemed as if there was nothing more that could be done. He told Caracciolo that Lorenzo was 'in a very bad way', 'traumatised by the things he had seen in Auschwitz,' and being 'an extremely sensitive man even though he almost never spoke about it,' had remained 'profoundly wounded and no longer wanted to live.'

Levi, on the other hand, had the feeling that he was already writing about a 'remote past'. *If This Is A Man* was published on 11 October 1947, less than two years after his return, although parts of it had appeared in the newspaper *L'amico del popolo* and the magazine *Il Ponte* between March and August of that year. As soon as he received the first copies of *If This Is A Man*, he took one to Lorenzo. He also took one to Bianca Guidetti Serra, who would keep hers; it bears the dedication: 'To Bianca, Primo'. We don't know what was written in the dedication to Lorenzo; perhaps something similar, perhaps something more. Unless it turns up some time in the future, Lorenzo's copy has been lost. After the death of her husband, Lorenzo's mother was very worn out, his brother Giovanni was 'almost entirely withdrawn' and Caterina, the 'proudest' of the family, became the de facto head of the family. It was Caterina who kept the photographs of Lorenzo as well as his work papers, 'because to her his work was Lorenzo, or the unspoilt part of him.' But she got rid of everything else: 'the mess tin in which he had taken his soup to Primo and Alberto; his clothes, including the white goatswool vest; his books, including his copy of *If This Is A Man* with Primo's dedication.'[11] She didn't throw Levi's letters away immediately, 'perhaps because they proved that someone else had loved Lorenzo' and had fought for him:

> But they also, therefore, proved something else: that he had been bent on self-destruction, that he was drinking himself to death. In the end the shame of Primo's letters grew greater than their consolation to Catarina, and to other upright, God-fearing Perones as well. Catarina herself, or one of the others, destroyed them some time later; just as, in 1945, Giovanna had burned Lorenzo's Auschwitz sack and everything in it. This is sad, of course, for biography. But it is sadder still for Lorenzo, and for his family.[12]

I have quoted extensively from Levi's public references to Lorenzo – both spoken and written – and perhaps it's only right that the memory of what was said privately has faded. Or else this is what we tell ourselves when something is irretrievably lost.

...

Having resigned from his work in Avigliana, in the lower Susa Valley, Primo Levi was leading a withdrawn life in his old home on Corso Re Umberto in Turin. He described himself as 'an extreme case of the sedentary person,'[13] apart from long excursions to the mountains and hills, his life was lived in the 'endless conversations in his sitting room, the very room where he had been born.'[14] Levi was a static, steady man, who had now become quite talkative. The opposite of Lorenzo, who had always been on the move and was now withdrawn into his pain and resentment. But he had not taken out that long-held anger, as old as history itself, on those weaker than himself. He had turned it into love, if I may be allowed the use of that immense word. This love runs in the lines handwritten by Lorenzo to Primo; the love that only a good man can feel.

The letter Lorenzo sends Primo from Fossano on 14 December 1947, on two sheets from an exercise book, is not yet desperate, but implies a never-ending sense of grief. If I read it well, he writes Auschwitz as 'Auschwiss,' and mentions 'lovely moments' he spent 'there' with his friend Primo. And he sends him a big hug, almost as if wanting one for himself, because 'it's better to forget'; the hair stands on end at that memory, but there isn't a single trace of anger:

Dear Signor Primo Levi.

I come with these few lines to let you know that I am well and I hope the same is true of you and your wife and your mamma I must tell you that the book you sent me I haven't been able to read yet because as soon as I received it it was ripped from my hands one person wanted to read it then another and I was the last but I hope that this week I'll also read it when you talk about Auschwiss my hair stands on end and it's better to forget sometimes I still dream at night about those lovely moments we spent there. with all this I send you best wishes for a good Christmas holiday for all of you in the family and here is a big hug from one who always remembers you your friend Lorenzo Perrone goodbye.

We have no idea if Lorenzo later read *If This Is A Man*. He would never again mention it in his letters, and what they might have said to each other about the book must remain a gap in this story. But some of the family must have spotted those passages in the chapters 'The Events of the Summer' and 'The Last One' where Lorenzo is mentioned.

I don't consider Lorenzo capable of the kind of vanity that would lead practically anyone else to look for himself in those pages, but I think it equally unlikely that he didn't know what his friend Primo had written about him, in those 250 lines (five printed pages in total) containing the essence of their story, a story that constantly reminded Levi that there was still 'a remote possibility of good, but for which it was worth surviving.'[15]

...

We mustn't fall into the trap of thinking that Primo Levi in 1947 was already the literary star we know of as Primo Levi. *If This Is A Man* was rejected by Einaudi publishing house, which reversed its decision several years later and printed a small number of copies: 2,000. Instead, the book was originally published by De Silva, and for the time, had only modest distribution. Levi would not acquire his reputation as a witness until the end of the 1950s, following Einaudi's reissue of the book in 1958. At the end of 1959 he twice made speeches in front of about 1,300 and 1,500 people, beginning a commitment that would become an intermittent but important part of his mission. But that was to come. Ten years earlier, the 1947 edition of *If This Is A*

Man, had basically circulated only via Levi's own circle, and not much beyond it:

> It was published for the first time in 1947, a run of 2,500 copies, and was well received by the critics but sold only in part: the six hundred unsold copies stored in Florence in a remainder warehouse were drowned in the autumn flood of 1969. After ten years of apparent death, it came back to life when the Einaudi publishing company accepted it in 1957. I have often asked myself a futile question: what would have happened if the book had immediately had a wide distribution? Perhaps nothing special: it is probable that I would have continued my hard-working life as a chemist who turned into a writer on Sunday (and not even every Sunday); or perhaps, on the other hand, I might have let myself be dazzled and, with who knows what luck, hoisted the banners of a life-sized writer. As I said, the question is futile: the business of reconstructing the hypothetical past, the what-would-have-happened-if is just as discredited as that of foreseeing the future.[16]

Levi wrote mainly to bear witness and to free himself of anguish, not to become a writer, although he was quite aware that he was taking a decisive step in that direction. But the question of 'what-would-have-happened-if' we can't help asking in the particular case of Lorenzo. Those 250 memorable lines, which tens, then hundreds of thousands of people would read from 1958 onwards, which are now a universal heritage, within reach of millions of readers in practically every corner of the globe, would have made Lorenzo a name. But as it was, while Lorenzo was alive, his actions, which throw an unexpected and almost blinding light on that grey planet, were only revealed to a few hundred people – and even they didn't know his face or surname.

...

I assume that Lorenzo and Primo saw less of each other from the spring of 1948 onwards. At the beginning of April, Primo started working tirelessly at SIVA – Società Industriale Vernici e Affini – a paint factory at 274 Corso Regina Margherita in Turin (which moved to Settimo Torinese in 1953), about five kilometres from where he lived, although his new workplace and the previous one in Avigliana were equidistant from Fossano. I would speculate that the main reason their encounters became less frequent was because Lucia was pregnant: on 1 October of that year their first child Lisa Lorenza was born – named, of course, after Lorenzo. And so Lorenzo sent Primo an affectionate Christmas card, with a snowy mountain landscape on one side and 'two lines for little Lisa Lorenza' on the other, 'wishing you a merry Christmas and a happy new year and may heaven be good to you goodbye. Lorenzo.' At the same time he also sent a letter – not a long one, but not short either. From it, we discover that he wasn't well: with the onset of winter, he was suffering from chronic bronchitis. The moment has come to take a deep breath and read the sweetest, most overwhelming testimony *by* – rather than *about* – Lorenzo that we have.

It is written in his own hand, two days before Christmas 1948, the first that his friend would live through as a father.

Dear Signor Dottor Primo

I am writing in reply to your letter it pleased me a lot to know that you still remember me and only I can't remember myself because when you are poor you will always be poor but this year I have been rich in health but you know how my illness is when I get to winter there's always a bit of bronchitis and I will have it until I die. I was very pleased to hear that two months ago your wife had a little girl the greatest gift you could give me was to call her Lisa Lorenza that way she will also carry my name but I hope thanking the Lord that she will not have to carry the suffering I have carried in my life. In the meantime please say hello for me to your wife and your Mamma and the whole family and also say hello for me to your friend De Benedetti. and I wish a merry christmas and a happy new year to your whole family and may you receive a sliver of the heart of one who will always remember you your friend Perrone Lorenzo goodbye

I must tell you that I would need many things but you have already done too many things for me and I am ashamed even to ask.

CHAPTER 12

And They Will Pay Back

I had hoped to find someone who had worked alongside Lorenzo still alive. The last company that hired him – on 13 September 1949, when Lorenzo had just turned forty-five, for an hourly pay of 45.60 lire – was called Antonio Dutto & Sons and was based in Spinetta, Cuneo. After dozens of telephone calls to various Duttos all over the region (where it's quite a common surname) and as I was ploughing through the city archives, I decided to launch, through the auspices of the local Chamber of Commerce, a kind of collective search, sharing on social media the seal of the company and the basic information I had gathered from fragments of conversations with assumed relatives and descendants. That's how I discovered that one of Antonio's two sons, Aldo, was nicknamed 'El Dutturin' (a nickname perhaps applied to the whole family). After some initial disappointments – none of the local builders remembered the firm – I learnt that El Dutturin's family are buried in the cemetery of the Spinetta district of Cuneo.

The bricklayer Antonio Dutto, a 'foreman' according to documentation until the early 1950s, when he began to define himself as a 'businessman', was eight years older than Lorenzo. Born in 1896 in Peveragno, some thirty kilometres from Fossano, he launched his activities twice. The first time was in Spinetta from 1931 until 1939, just over two months before the outbreak of the Second World

War. The second time was in 1946, while he was repairing a building he owned that had been damaged during the war. In September 1950 the business moved to Cuneo. It never seems to have officially closed, but it's possible that the Register of Companies automatically annulled it on the death of the owner, which occurred in 1958. It was this second company that was operating in 1949 on a site in Fossano and which hired Lorenzo, as shown by a rubber stamp on his employment record. The signature on it is Aldo's: this much we can deduce if we compare it with the signature on paperwork from the same year relating to the extension of a family property. This was a period when thanks to the Fanfani Plan which aimed at building houses for the workers, the Fossano newspaper *La Fedeltà* was rejoicing at the opening of new sites, which would bring 'a significant amount of work that will alleviate unemployment.'

But there is nobody – Antonio's sons, who we assume were working with him in 1949, having also died – who remembers Lorenzo. Apart from Antonio, who died the year Einaudi brought out the new edition of *If This Is A Man*, his sons Aldo – 'El Dutturin' – and Oreste passed away in 2002 and 2020 respectively: the family tomb in Spinetta leaves no room for doubt (their sister, Caterina, died in 2008). It was admittedly a faint hope to find someone who was in their twenties at the time – in their late nineties today – who had any memory of Lorenzo.

From a quarrel involving his neighbours in the area of Tetti Bovis and the technical office of the municipality of Cuneo, centred on the building of some woodsheds, which dragged on for more than a year, it seems that Antonio Dutto was a persuasive talker. I don't know if or how he persuaded Lorenzo to work for him, or how Lorenzo on the contrary decided to ask him for the chance. All I know for certain, as Dutto, having plenty of experience as both a foreman and a boss, doubtless also knew, is that he agreed to hire a vagrant.

...

Lorenzo was ill, as he wrote to Primo at Christmas 1948: 'you know how my illness is when I get to winter there's always a bit of bronchitis and I will have it until I die.' It's possible that at the end of 1949, when he had been working for Antonio Dutto & Sons for two months and another winter arrived, he had a relapse. What is certain is that on 14 January 1950, four months after being hired for the Fossano site, he was again registered as unemployed. There is no major documentation making it possible to properly reconstruct the last two years of Lorenzo's life, except the words of Primo and the memories of others. I know that at least once he went to see Levi, and not vice-versa, as his wife Lucia recalled. Let us start with those who really knew him.

In an interview from 1978 (which appeared posthumously), Levi maintains that Lorenzo no longer wanted to live. Levi also said that Lorenzo had returned home 'much more desperate than me', that he was 'terrified by what he had seen, scared, wounded', and that he had contracted tuberculosis. In 'Lorenzo's Return' (from 1981, let us remember) he wrote simply, without further details, that 'he fell ill', adding nevertheless that 'thanks to some physician friends of mine I was able to get him into a hospital, but they gave him no wine and he ran away.'[1] In another interview from 1983 Levi confirms the disease was tuberculosis. 'He fell ill with tuberculosis,' he told Motola in 1985 and Rosenfeld in 1986; and to the latter he referred to what he had written five years earlier, adding a dramatic reference to his own powerlessness: 'they sent him to the hospital, but there they didn't give him wine, and so he ran away. I tried to help him get well, but in vain.' In the interview with Caracciolo, also from 1986, he specifies the hospital: 'he would get drunk and sleep in the open air – he had caught pneumonia – I had him admitted to the hospital in Savigliano, but they didn't give him wine, and he ran away, and they later found him dying in a canal, where he had fallen asleep drunk.'

In the decade before his own death, Levi gave by far the largest number of interviews in his life – most of them were published posthumously – and in them he often repeated himself and also started to fear that he was losing his memory. But he sets down all the essential elements that would help his readers learn what had happened to Lorenzo. Only precise dates are missing. So we learn that Lorenzo fell ill with tuberculosis – but did it begin with pneumonia? Or vice-versa? And what about the bronchitis he wrote to Primo about? We also learn that he was hospitalised thanks to Primo's doctor friends in nearby Savigliano but ran away from there because he needed to drink. Unfortunately, there is no way of verifying this information, seventy years later. Although at the time the hospital in Savigliano had one of the few departments in the region equipped for tuberculosis patients, Lorenzo's medical record, which would be most valuable, is literally untraceable, and might even never have existed: it was only following the Mariotti reform of 1968–9 that doctors kept obligatory records. And, by the way, who were these friends in Savigliano? I've been unable to find out. Sometimes that's how it ends, and you find yourself having to condense months of fruitless research that has involved archivists and civil servants – at least six in this case – and cost them God knows how many hours of work, into a meagre paragraph.

So, when did Lorenzo's clinical history begin, his gradual slide towards an increasingly chronic, desperate condition? In this interview Fossano librarian Carlo Morra said Lorenzo was already a sick *ciucatun* (a drunkard) from 1950 or 1951:

> My memories of Lorenzo Perone are few and by now also faded. I met him, I think it was 1950 or 1951, together with an uncle of mine who must have worked occasionally with him. To a request of mine as to who that down-at-heel man was, I was told that he was a bricklayer, that he was ill, and by now wasn't working much and would be more likely to find in the tavern.
>
> Naturally my memory is more than vague and is mixed up with what I read subsequently by Primo Levi.[2]

Even though he had no specific memory of Lorenzo, who was one of the many patients going in and out of the tuberculosis ward, Dr Giovanni Niffenegger, born in 1927, began to work occasionally in the hospital in Savigliano in 1950, taking up a permanent position there two years later. 'These are memories of my youth, they are still vivid,' he tells me. 'I went there many times,' he sighs, recalling the tuberculosis patients who 'came and went' and who 'emitted millions of bacilli' – particularly vivid to him are the deaths of a nurse and of a nun, both infected by patients.[3]

Mayor Manfredi, who was between nineteen and twenty-five at the time of Lorenzo's 'return' (for him, as for Morra, it was always Perone with one 'r'), would recall in the early 1990s that during that phase of his life Lorenzo went from one tavern to another until they actually stopped serving him. He ran away 'along the banks of Salmour' until he was 'found almost dead', and that at this point Levi 'had him transported to the hospital in Savigliano where he had acquaintances' – probably borrowing, at least partly, what Levi himself had stated not long before.

Still in the 1990s, independently and with equal tenacity, Thomson and Angier set about trying to reconstruct the last months of Lorenzo's life. Thomson wrote that he had contracted 'tuberculosis aggravated by bronchial pneumonia', and in this case, corroborated by what Lorenzo wrote to Levi at the end of 1948, the information 'disseminated' subsequently by Levi would be corrected. In his archive preserved in the Wiener Holocaust Library in London, which holds his birth and baptism certificates, there is no document reporting the cause of death. Thomson nevertheless managed to gain one further insight of value:

> One night, fired with grape brandy, Lorenzo fell in with an ex-policeman named Araglia who was homeless and, it turned out, tubercular. Perrone invited him home for more drink and the policeman slept rough on the floor with Perrone's five brothers and sisters. Inevitably Perrone's alcoholism made him susceptible to the tuberculosis, and within weeks he had begun to cough blood. Levi managed to find him a bed in Savigliano Hospital not far from Fossano, where he knew a doctor. There he bought the mason wool jumpers, a new pair of winter trousers, and sat by his bed holding his hand. Perrone began to hallucinate rats and lions and, according to his brother Secondo, 'winged beasts.'[4]

Alcoholism and tuberculosis often manifest simultaneously in the same patient. In the past it was believed that the causes of both were to be sought in poverty and in precarious life conditions; today we tend to emphasise the very narrow relationship between them. While it is true that alcoholism sometimes develops in a patient as a way of alleviating the pain caused by tuberculosis, in the case of Lorenzo it was already well established by the time he contracted the disease. For decades now we have known that, where tuberculosis and alcoholism are both present, 'it is necessary for the phthisiologist, the psychiatrist or the alcohologist to act in close collaboration.'[5] Where alcoholism is present, the immune system is under a lot of pressure, and this was clearly the case with Lorenzo, already afflicted with chronic bronchitis even before contracting tubercolosis. Ethanol interferes with the normal functioning of various components of the immune system, leading to immune deficiency and increasing susceptibility to certain infections: in particular, at the time, pneumonia and tuberculosis. It's a vicious circle and Lorenzo ended up in the middle of it. Thanks to the legislation of 1913 and 1923 alcoholism was now recognised as a disease, although, on account of a long history of criminal anthropology, habitual drinkers were still considered individuals to be punished. Since Lorenzo was perfectly capable of hurting himself, it wasn't necessary for anybody else to punish him.

It may be ungenerous to say that Lorenzo was deliberately looking for his own death, even though the secondary sources in our possession, almost without exception, suggest this reading of events. Only Morra might make us hesitate, and Levi himself would write in his story 'In Due Time': 'it's not a given that someone who is tired of life, or says he is, always want to die: in general, he only wants a better life.' But was Lorenzo allowing himself to harbour some hope in a better life? Where is the line between resisting illness and allowing oneself to deteriorate, poisoning oneself day after day with cynical determination? Angier writes:

> He was poor again, he could help no one; it was he who needed help now. And as though to make the point doubly clear, it was Primo who helped him. Primo gave as naturally and silently as Lorenzo had done; he would have repeated that he was not giving but giving back, and even if he gave back all his life he would still be in debt to Lorenzo ... The only thing [Lorenzo] could do about help was refuse it. So that is what he did.[6]

Levi visited him every week in hospital. Angier offers us some further heartbreaking details from the family memory, including how 'his brothers came often, his younger sister [Giovanna] came from Turin, Caterina came almost every day. But he was not allowed drink in the hospital; and as soon as he could he ran away.'[7] This is confirmed for me by his niece Emma, who remembers those months vividly – she was fourteen – and, surprisingly, removes any ambiguity about Levi's mysterious contact in Savigliano: it was the brothers, Michele and Secondo, who had Lorenzo admitted to hospital, not Levi. The proud Caterina would not have appreciated this narrative 'rounding out', which might imply that the family had not bothered with him. Perhaps Levi wanted, on the contrary, to accentuate his own responsibilities.

'A lot of them did that "job" of running away, unfortunately,' Dr Niffenegger confesses to me, going back to the memories of his twenty-five years, his tone wonderfully empathetic. So Lorenzo returned home, 'where he must have been received with dismay – he was highly infectious, he had left the hospital illegally, and he was desperate for wine.'[8] This is how Angier tells it; in reality, a big meal was laid on to celebrate his return, Emma tells me emotionally. The family members – to return to Angier's account – 'contacted Primo, who wanted to have him brought to Turin. For the last time, Lorenzo refused. In the end the family notified the Savignano hospital and Lorenzo was returned.'[9] It was the brothers who took him back, and in those sad weeks they went back and forth to Savigliano by Vespa, to look after him. His accommodation was more than respectable, with a bed all of his own, but there was little to be done now. Manfredi also remembered that he 'was visited considerately and helped' by his brothers and sisters, and that 'he carried' what he had seen and felt 'locked away inside himself as if in a tomb.' But what's particularly painful is that it was his own family that made him go back into hospital – for his own good, obviously, and everyone else's. His was a nomadic, vagabond soul, and I say this with love and respect.

Don Lenta is a name that recurs in the work of both Angier and Thomson. He was a crucial figure in the memories left by a wandering life. A contemporary of Levi (he was born at the beginning of 1919), Carlo Lenta became a priest in 1942, a month after Lorenzo arrived in Buna. By the time Lorenzo returned home, Lenta was deputy priest at the Cathedral of Fossano, and on 1 May 1951 he became chaplain of the city hospital. He was also the author of a number of pamphlets denouncing 'the dominance and exploitation of man by man;' he was a 'righteous priest' who would devote his life to the sick for over five decades, until his death on 30 April 2003. Thomson, who interviewed him ten years earlier, when Lenta was seventy-four, doesn't remember him as being so old: he was very kind, very patient, extremely attached to 'his' people. He was 'a very decent man',[10] he tells me, who had seen Lorenzo as the symbol of a vanishing world, or rather, of a vanishing way of seeing life.

His moving and untiring commitment to remembering the odyssey of that lost soul demonstrates this well. This is the same Don Lenta who, in 1982, claimed proudly in the newspaper *La Fedeltà* that 'in the suggestive pages of the famous writer's latest collection', in other words, in *Moments of Reprieve*, there was 'a bricklayer from the Borgo Vecchio of Fossano;' the same Don Lenta who in 1993 gave Thomson the last images of a Lorenzo selling scrap metal in the snow, blue in the face, and who told him that in those days 'the bricklayers and fishermen of Fossano went out of their way to help the weakest in the community'; the same Don Lenta who two years later, after conducting 'research among the elderly inhabitants of Fossano, including those who had been entrepreneurs and bricklayers in the Borgo Vecchio before the war,' would report that in the period after his homecoming Lorenzo worked as a scrap merchant like his father; and last but not least, the same Don Lenta who, on 22 January 1997, from Fossano, on headed notepaper from the hospital in Savigliano, provided Angier with valuable testimony about Lorenzo's death, which brought forward the procedure for conferring on him the title of 'Righteous Among the Nations'. 'In the end Lorenzo contrived his own abandonment; no one could save him – not even Primo Levi,'[11] Don Lenta summarises.

Perhaps it was the slaves who had temporarily saved Lorenzo, giving him a purpose, a mission. Perhaps Lorenzo wanted to help more and didn't succeed. It is hard not to recall the famous final scene of *Schindler's List*, in which the protagonist's desperation unexpectedly erupts at the thought that he could, *should*, have done more. 'I could have got more out,' Schindler says, weeping, 'I didn't do enough,' he insists desperately, on his knees. A passage in the Talmud that says that whoever saves a life saves the whole world. And yet that's the way it is for saviours who bear the burden of survival.

So this is what happened: Lorenzo was not saved.

After six months of toing and froing between admission and discharge, escape and return, at about 7.00pm on Wednesday 30 April 1952, Lorenzo died.

...

Rain had been falling for days, perhaps for weeks, by 30 April of that year during the long post-war period. In the local newspapers there are even references to hailstorms, as well as to 'torrential' rains that marked the spring. The feast of San Giovenale, the patron saint of Fossano, was approaching, and there were reports that new public lighting would usher the city into the modern world; but there were also days when drunken brawls continued to fill the columns of the local press.

The only mention of Lorenzo's death appears in the pages of the weekly *Il Popolo Fossanese*, which expresses 'sincere condolences to the Perrone family [,] in particular to our friend Michele, for the death of their relative Lorenzo Perrone on the evening of 30 April, at the age of forty-eight'. Actually, Lorenzo did not even reach that age: he would have turned forty-eight in September, if he had lived.

Life, in any case, would carry on, with its joys and sorrows. In Fossano between 25 April and 1 May, as well as five births, the deaths of three women were registered, respectively sixty-seven, seventy-six and seventy-eight years of age, followed in the next few days by a manual labourer of ninety-one and a stoker of fifty-four, while a sick fourteen-year-old boy passed away tragically in Villafalletto.

Although his political consciousness was probably quite confused, Lorenzo was closer to the anarchist murdered in the United States twenty-five years earlier than to many of his fellow citizens who went to church every Sunday. Levi described him (with a few exceptions, as in this sentence, which may have been transcribed erroneously: 'he was a very mild and very pious man, rough and at the same time religious') as non-religious, a non-believer, while Don Lenta would attribute this position of his to his return from 'Suiss'. And yet the death certificate issued by the parish church of Santa Maria della Pieve, opposite the hospital of Savigliano, states that he was 'fortified by the Sacraments', and the fact that it was signed by the then parish priest Francesco Marengo implies strongly that Lorenzo was given the last rites. But there is nothing else, apart from the hour of death. At the city's register office, the data is even more basic and bureaucratic: a confirmation of the place and of the fact that he was unmarried.

Don Lenta's testimony, as released for the Yad Vashem file, is crucial. In it, he states that 'Signor Lorenzo Perone of Fossano, who died in the hospital of Savigliano on 30 April 1952 had a civil burial in Fossano on 2 May and [was] buried in plot 569 of the cemetery of the same city.' There is no reason to doubt him: it would have been within Don Lenta's remit to remember a religious ceremony, if it had happened. He adds, though, that Lorenzo was bidden farewell by the community, not in the church, as Emma remembers, but outside, strange perhaps but not so unusual.

Outside the church of San Giorgio in Via Garibaldi – where the body was laid out after being brought from Savigliano – Primo Levi spoke, publicly reiterating his gratitude to the late Lorenzo, commemorated in his writings as 'Signor Lorenzo', who had saved his life between June and December 1944 in the camp of Buna-Monowitz (Auschwitz III).

I swear to this,
Carlo Lenta, priest.

Needless to say, I've tried in every way possible to discover what exactly Levi said on that occasion. I know that he said only a few words, repeating what he would say on other occasions: 'I believe that I owe my being alive today to Lorenzo.' But as far as I know, none of those present kept a diary. Besides, as it was a civil ceremony, no documentation about it has reached us, except for the testimonies of those who were present or who were interviewed in the following decades. On the other hand, there is no trace of any religious ceremony in any of the parishes in Fossano, including San Giorgio, although Thomson mentions that 'a wake was held at 14 Via Michelini,' in the house where he was born, that same 30 April, 'followed by obsequies in San Giorgio church,'[12] probably referring to that civil ceremony which involved much of the *Burgué*, and which may have extended inside the building, as Emma's clearly remembers.

If in 1952 Levi had already become the Levi that the world would get to know between the 1960s and the 1980s, that is, if he had already started to become famous, everything would have been easier, clearer. 'How resist the fascination of bifurcated paths?'[13] Instead, the path we have through the last weeks of Lorenzo's life is a tangled web. We have a few heartrending images, such as that of Lorenzo's five siblings who 'stood in silence as Levi placed flowers on the open coffin.'[14] In those same years when Don Lenta went back to the memory of Lorenzo and Thomson and Angier tried to sketch his story, Mayor Manfredi remembered that Lorenzo's body 'was transferred from Savigliano to the Church of San Giorgio, in the Borgo Vecchio, where the Perones lived; and many people came to the funeral, including, in the front row, Primo Levi, his wife and their daughter' (although Emma, who saw Levi at the station, doesn't recall there being a little girl with them). Manfredi added that his family members remembered that Levi 'was dressed in a white sweater' (his source was Secondo's wife). 'And in this little detail,' he would write, 'there is all the affection the family bore this extraordinary man whom Levi's pen has made eternal and universal.'[15]

And yet Lorenzo died in despair, and even after his death, from what his family had been able to see, his attempts to save his own life failed. For this reason, according to Angier, 'to the Perones Lorenzo's death was not a martyrdom; it was a family tragedy, and a family shame.'[16]

...

On the Gothic spring day when I go to the cemetery of Fossano to look for plot 569, seventy years and a few days after Lorenzo's death, I discover that he died a Perrone, with two 'r's. I go back there on a sun-drenched, sweltering summer afternoon, to take a closer look. The gravestone is eroded, Lorenzo's name can barely be made out. His aunt was buried later in the same plot, and looming in place of Lorenzo's name is the name of the widow of his uncle, who shared Lorenzo's name and who was also his godfather. 'That' Lorenzo Perrone, who was dead when his nephew returned from military service, has a merry face: his pose is austere but not repellent, and there's a glimpse of a half-smile beneath the moustache.

In the family tomb, where Lorenzo was transferred more than twenty years later and 'transformed' into a Perone with a single 'r' (like every blood relative buried there), alongside his portrait from his time in military service there are portraits of practically all the family members: his father and his mother, who died less than nine months later, Giovanni (d. 1976), Caterina (d. 1992), Giovanna (d. 1979) and Michele (d. 1988); only Secondo is missing. All the siblings buried there died between twenty-three and fifty years after Lorenzo, and only the dour Giuseppe preceded him.

Thinking again about Lorenzo's two burials preceded by a secular community ritual and by a death in solitude but surrounded by brothers and sisters, and Primo who, in the following months would appear 'drawn and pale, and grieving for his friend;'[17] I turn back to that farewell amid the ruins of the Third Reich, when Lorenzo had a perforated eardrum, gifting over the patched-up vest; the postcards to Bianca that ended with 'Goodbye – *ciau*'; to the *menaschka* that for six months was always full; to the 'lovely moments we spent there;' to the dawn encounter amid the rubble, almost eight years earlier, hearing the first few words uttered in Piedmont dialect in the grey Planet Auschwitz, 1,412 kilometres from home.

I can't think Levi's appearance as he made his final farewell to Lorenzo, when he arrived at the funeral with his wife and perhaps little Lisa Lorenza, who was now three and a half years old, was as random as it sounds. He was wearing a white sweater at a funeral. Perhaps it was a tribute to that warm, uncomfortable goat's wool vest which was the first thing Primo took his friend Lorenzo at the end of his 'truce' late in the year 1945. Or perhaps it was just a nod to an unconventional patch of light in the black hole of twentieth-century history.

PART V

[…] 'pain cannot be taken away, it shouldn't be, because it is our guardian. He is often a foolish guardian, because he is inflexible, he is faithful to his delivery with maniacal obstinacy, and he never gets tired, while all other sensations get tired, wear out, especially the pleasant ones. But you cannot suppress it, silence it, because it is one with life. It is its guardian.'

— Primo Levi, 'Versamina'

CHAPTER 13

The Story of a Holy Drinker[1]

On more than a few occasions, Primo Levi would go so far as to maintain that Lorenzo's death was suicide. This is something he would declare in interviews starting in the 1980s, not long before his own death by suicide in 1987. If such was the case, 'his' Don Quixote would have been one of at least eleven suicides that Levi knew well: they include his German teacher at the Goethe, Hans Dieter Engert, whom my father remembers with enormous affection.

In 1978 Levi limited himself to remarking that Lorenzo 'died of TB, and unhappy.' Three years later, in 'Lorenzo's Return', he implicitly maintained the theory of suicide: 'he was assured and coherent in his rejection of life,' he writes. 'He, who was not a survivor, had died of the survivors' disease.'[2] This is the ending of 'Lorenzo's Return', and Levi would use these exact words, with minimal variations, whenever he again spoke of his friend's death, verbally or in writing, making his reading of the events increasingly manifest. In a 1993 interview we even read a dialogue reported by him: 'to those who, like me, said to him: "why are you killing yourself?" he would say, "oh yes, I'm killing myself." And he died later of TB because he would get drunk and sleep in the open, he'd lost the will to live. Perhaps because of what he'd seen ... but it's very hard to find an explanation for such a solitary man.' Two years later, in 1985, Levi told Motola, 'he was afraid of the world. Seeing people dying like flies in Auschwitz had made him an unhappy man. He wasn't a Jew, nor had he been a prisoner. But he was very sensitive. [...] He died of drink and TB. Yes. It was a genuine suicide.'

But does that mean that we should accept it as suicide? He himself claimed it was, according to what Primo reported, and there is no reason to doubt that. I think that the reflections in Levi's last book, *The Drowned and the Saved*, written between the end of the 1970s and the middle of the 1980s, although they refer to the deported, describe distinctly what happened to Lorenzo too: it was the 'turning to look back' that caused many cases of suicide after the liberation, when 'the awareness emerged that we had not done anything, or not enough,'[3] and almost everyone felt 'guilty of having omitted to offer help,' even when it wasn't true. The inability to stop such contagious, total evil, that 'concrete, heavy, perennial' shame, gnawed away at everyone; but those whom Levi would describe as 'the just among us' also lived another, particularly excruciating kind of shame:

> [The just among us] neither more nor less numerous than in any other human group, felt remorse, shame and pain for the misdeeds that others and not they had committed, and in which they felt involved, because they sensed that what had happened around them in their presence, and in them, was irrevocable. It would never again be able to be cleansed; it would prove that man, the human species – we, in short – were potentially able to construct an infinite enormity of pain; and that pain is the only force that is created from nothing, without cost and without effort. It is enough not to see, not to listen, not to act.[4]

The 'shame of the world', as much as unjust but relentless personal shame, could lead to suicide. We must treat this matter with great care and caution. Levi's perhaps most cited words on the theme, much investigated by scholars because of his own tragic death, are those he wrote on the occasion of the suicide of Jean Améry – real name Hans Chaim Mayer – an Austrian Jewish partisan and Auschwitz survivor who killed himself in 1978, at his second attempt. In an article in *La Stampa*, Levi insists on the complex nature of this extreme gesture. 'It is particularly difficult to penetrate the reasoning of a suicide, since, in general, the suicide himself is not aware of it, or else provides himself and others with motives that are wittingly and unwittingly false.' In the chapter of *The Drowned and the Saved* devoted to Améry, Levi writes that all suicides admit 'a nebula of explanations.' Levi could also be speaking of Lorenzo: 'those who "trade blows" with the entire world achieve dignity but pay a very high price for it, because they are sure to be defeated.'[5]

Can we consider Lorenzo's 'letting go,' accelerated as it clearly was by extreme alcohol abuse, a gesture that could be defined as a 'voluntary death,' to quote the subtitle of Améry's book *On Suicide* (published in 1976, two years after his previous attempt and two years before his final, successful one)? I find a possible answer to this painful and impenetrable question in Thomas Macho's weighty tome *Das Leben nehmen: Suizid in der Moderne*. Although it has been observed that the increase in suicide in the century before Lorenzo's death was due to industrialisation, increasing poverty, the ever-higher cost of living, the shortage of housing, alcoholism and tuberculosis – all matters which more or less directly impinge on Lorenzo – recent statistics reveal a further significant increase in the practice, initially among the 'defeated' combatants at the end of a conflict like the Second World War. And all the evidence points to the fact that, between 1945 and 1952, Lorenzo was indeed, in a broad sense, a defeated man.

In the same year, 1976, the philosopher Wilhelm Kamlah proposed giving a socially recognised form to 'the right to one's own death'. Macho observes that 'suicide out of necessity, justified by age, solitude, an incurable disease or unbearable pain, is today generally respected and passive euthanasia is admitted in almost all European countries', and goes on to explore the specific theme of martyrdom and 'political suicide'. This, I think, is the point. 'Suicide as a form of political protest is a kind of continuation of martyrdom by other means,' Macho concludes. Referring to the 'human torches' of the 1960s, he draws a convincing comparison between suicide by fire and the refusal of food, 'a kind of slow inner fire.' It is a reading that Macho situates within the broader history of 'cultures of radical refusal.' And here, for a fleeting moment, I seem to grasp at least partly the reason for Lorenzo's slow and inexorable withdrawal from the world: the sentence 'to live no longer interested him'[6] that has been bouncing around in my head for years, written by Levi in *Moments of Reprieve* in discussing his friend's overwhelming desire to 'get away from the world.' Like Shalom Aleichem's milkman Tevye, often quoted by Levi, Lorenzo was 'a simple man,' but he had 'a high and noble ideal of the life of man on earth.'[7] He had fought with all his strength and, in an extreme gesture of protest, had then decided, more or less consciously, to leave it.

...

In the chapter 'The Grey Zone' of *The Drowned and the Saved*, his 'spiritual testament' and 'moral book', Levi wrote that 'an infernal order such as National Socialism, exercises a frightful power of corruption, against which it is difficult to guard oneself. It degrades its victims and makes them similar to itself, because it needs both great and small complicities. To resist it a truly solid moral armature is needed.'[8] Earlier in the same book, he writes that 'the ascent of the privileged, not only in the Lager but in all human coexistence, is an anguishing but unfailing phenomenon: only in Utopias are they absent. It is the duty of righteous men to make war on all undeserved privilege, but one must not forget that this is a war without end.'[9]

On the margins of that 'cruel laboratory' that was the Lager, that righteous man had existed, his name was Lorenzo, and he had fought his battle, and been crushed. The drama of the 'just man oppressed by injustice' was one of the pillars of Levi's whole life, not only in his work. It was not by chance that he chose to open his personal anthology *The Search for Roots* with the case of Job, present in the Jewish and Christian Bible as the archetype of the 'righteous' man. In Levi's words:

> This magnificent and harrowing story encapsulates the questions of all the ages, those for which man has never to this day found an answer, nor will he ever find one, but he will always search for it because he needs it in order to live, to understand himself and the world. Job is the just man oppressed by injustice. He is the victim of a cruel wager between Satan and God: what will Job – pious, healthy, rich and happy – do if he is deprived of his wealth, deprived of family love, and finally assailed

under his own skin? Well then, Job the Just, degraded to an animal for an experiment, comports himself as any of us would, at first he lowers his head and praises God ('Shall we receive good at the hand of God, and shall we not receive evil?'), then his defences collapse. Poor, bereft of his children, covered in boils, he sits among the ashes, scratching himself with a potsherd, and contends with God.[10]

In the story 'Renzo's Fist' in *Other People's Trades*, Levi names the enigma over which characters like Job 'tormented themselves': 'the reason for evil.'[11] They do not accept suffering and go so far as to deny God, he insisted in an interview. God or no God, Levi's testimony and reflection would always interrogate common humanity. And in the Lager 'the just man behaved as a just man,' as he said in another interview. When it came down to it, even in that twisted, unfathomable context, it was really quite simple. When humanity is revealed, it is like when we develop a photograph. In the copious 'sample book that Auschwitz had placed open'[12] before Levi, Lorenzo had shown himself to be a pure man, like an owl at ease in the dark but confused in sunlight. We've already seen the desperation showing through the words he wrote to his friend Primo at the time of his homecoming in that heartbreaking letter, and to give them greater solidity we cannot help but recall the opening of *The Truce* – an opening that might have been written as early as 1947 and was partly quoted by Levi himself in his last book. Here, he describes four young Russians on horseback, dazed, traumatised and paralysed by the sight of the Lager 'packed with corpses and dying persons.'[13]

> They did not greet us, nor did they smile; they seemed oppressed not only by compassion but by a confused restraint, which sealed their lips and bound their eyes to the funereal silence. It was that shame we knew so well, the shame that drowned us after the selections, and every time we had to watch, or submit to, some outrage ... So for us even the hour of liberty rang out grave and muffled, and filled our souls with joy and yet with a painful sense of pudency, so that we should have liked to wash our consciences and our memories clean from the foulness that lay upon them; and also with anguish, because we felt that this should never happen, that now nothing could ever happen good and pure enough to rub out our past, and that the scars of the outrage would remain within us for ever.[14]

Levi went much further, as a non-believer, in talking about Lorenzo. The epithet of 'Saint Anthony' was not only a tender *boutade*. In 1981 he described him 'as a saviour who's come from heaven.'[15] In the posthumously published *The Paris Review* interview he declared that Lorenzo was 'really a sort of a saint,' but already in 1975, six years before publishing 'Lorenzo's Return', Levi hinted at the theme of sainthood in an interview with Corrado Stajano published in *Il Giorno*. The question was, 'in the Lager, what were the rules for survival?'

> There is a reverse debate between me and the readers of my book, who consider that I survived thanks to my self-control, my moral strength. These things contributed 10 per cent to my salvation, in truth I was saved because of my health (I weighed forty-eight kilos,

one eats in proportion to one's weight, at the liberation I weighed forty-two), because I'd had training in physical effort (mountaineering, cycling), because I had been admitted to the chemical lab (I was given small privileges), and because of the help of Lorenzo, a bricklayer from Fossano. He was a simple man, a saint, it seemed to him obvious that he should help the suffering without compensation. Later, he didn't want to be saved by anyone and he died eradicated by the world, in 1950.

In this text we find a dating error, bringing the date of his friend's death forward by two years. In 1986, not long before his own death, in the conversation with Rosenfeld, Levi would again insist on Lorenzo's saintliness – and again get the date wrong: 'he'd lost the will to live and so he died, in 1947. He was a man alone. In my opinion, even though he wasn't a religious man, he was a saint.' In the last twelve years of his life, then, Levi antedated Lorenzo's death, first by two years, then by five.

It's highly unlikely that he did not remember the developments in his own life in the second half of the 1940s: the first edition of *If This Is A Man*, his marriage, the birth of Lisa Lorenza, his work at SIVA. Could these two errors be the fault of the editors, not the author? What Primo wrote about Lorenzo was always highly guarded; plus, we have no audio-visual records of these two interviews, unlike the one with Caracciolo. Although Levi was not infallible as a human being, in these cases his accounts were filtered through other hands: what he wrote, or intended, should be treated differently compared with what he is presumed to have said.

And yet one image dominates: at the time of his homecoming, the time of those letters from 1947 and 1948, Lorenzo perhaps appeared as if he'd already been given up for dead.

CHAPTER 14

The Last Word

For Levi, 1952 was only the beginning. A few weeks after Lorenzo's death, on 16 July 1952, the publisher Einaudi showed renewed interest in *If This Is A Man*, although it would be another three years before the contract was signed. The new edition was finally published on 9 May 1958, by which time Levi's second child, Renzo, born in July 1957, was almost a year old.

Even though he had seen Lorenzo many times between the first and second editions of *If This Is A Man*, Levi decided to make almost no changes in what he had written about their relationship in Auschwitz. After a few translations of *If This Is A Man*, including the German one (*Ist das ein Mensch?*) in 1961, its sequel, *The Truce*, was published on April 1 1963. From then on, *If This Is A Man* was frequently reissued, becoming one of the most widely read books of the post-war period and confirming Levi's mounting fame in Italy, setting him on a path that would see him proclaimed the 'witness per excellence,' a kind of 'guru' of memory – an epithet he always rejected.

During the 1960s, Levi still went back to Fossano to meet Lorenzo's family. And on 18 September 1979, having heard about the death of Giovanna Perrone, he wrote a moving letter to her daughter Emma, Lorenzo's niece:

THE LAST WORD

Dear Signora,

I remember your mother very well, having contacted her several times in order to have news of Lorenzo and to keep in touch with him. It grieves me to know that she is no longer with us and that she suffered so much, and I share your grief: when we love someone, their death always seems like a great injustice. I am grateful to you for writing to me: I've never forgotten Lorenzo, and if I have the opportunity to pass through Fossano, I will go and say hello to him where he rests beside his brothers.

Primo Levi with his son Renzo, 1959.

In the 1980s, starting with the American translation of *The Periodic Table* and the 'explosion of interest' that followed, Levi became famous internationally. By 1985 *If This Is A Man* had been translated into nine languages. In Italy alone it had sold more than half a million copies and there was talk of a possible Nobel Prize. These were the very years in which Levi would again reflect on his 'salvation'. As we have seen, he returned several times to Lorenzo's story: in the stage version of *If This Is A Man* in 1966–7, where Lorenzo literally comes back to life; in 'Lorenzo's Return' in 1981; and finally in *The Drowned and the Saved* in 1986. There were also the various interviews, especially in the 1980s and above all in the last few years of his life, in which he would add the odd detail about the 'bricklayer who brought me food,' 'a marginal man' whom he would go so far as to describe as an 'anarchist', in almost Lombrosian terms – meaning, I suppose, that he was a 'rebel', one of those who do not bow their head when faced with the injustices of society but act accordingly.

Thanks to the interview given to Rosenfeld a year before he died, which Angier, unsurprisingly, would include in the documentation for Yad Vashem, we know at least the nationalities of other slave labourers helped by Lorenzo: on that occasion, Levi said that Lorenzo had helped 'two or three other prisoners, non-Italians: a Frenchman, a Pole and so on.' By the time he gave this interview he was a world-famous author, and he knew that perfectly well.

There was not much time left. On 11 April 1987 Levi fell down the stairs in his apartment building on Corso Re Umberto in Turin. His fame grew constantly in the following decades. In 2015 *The Complete Works of Primo Levi* made Levi the first Italian author whose entire output is available in English. A few years earlier – as Thomson observes in the reissue of his biography, published in 2019 on the occasion of Levi's centenary – he had literally become a star: a small planet had been named after him, Primolevi, all one word.

Until the last days of his life, Primo never stopped asking himself why he should have survived, swinging between various unverifiable calculations of percentages, but remaining always steadfast on the 'triptych' comprising good luck, ability and prevarication. Lorenzo had supplied him with the explanation he was looking for: he allowed him to place himself among the luckiest, and not among the worst; he was also skilful, and his 'complicity in the guilt' was minimal; he himself, implicitly, did not condemn himself. And this thanks to the luck of meeting Lorenzo. Because that's what it was. Luck, pure luck. The first noun in *If This Is A Man* is 'fortune.' Which some called and still call 'providence'.

...

I remember a trip to the cinema with my father to see Francesco Rosi's film *The Truce* in 1997, the year of its release. I was fourteen. Presumably I had already read the book and, at least once, *If This Is A Man*. Like many of the generations born after the war, I grew up on Levi's works, starting with those two, which I read several times from middle school onwards several times. Later (much too late: it must have been 2008) came *The Drowned and the Saved*, and then gradually all the rest. A life spent reading and rereading Levi, caught up by that mixture of testimony, literature and 'anthropological investigation' – ethological, we might almost say: he himself insisted a great deal on the fact that he was an example of the 'human animal'. And yet I myself have no memory of coming across Lorenzo, either as a child or a teenager. This is an observation made worse by the fact that my father actually had the good luck to attend a German course at the Goethe Institut with Levi just before I was born (Levi attended for five years, from the end of 1978), sometimes even giving him a lift in his car in 1980–1, and frequently told me about it.

I became aware of Lorenzo only much later. I still wonder why this story went under the radar of the collective consciousness, even though Levi's work is strewn with references to this man of few words driven 'by an uncontrollable impulse' to help those who needed help. As if he were simply a minor character in the story, rather than the one who made it possible. 'It was technically impossible' to survive without 'external help', as Levi said, in June 1986.

Some fifteen printed pages don't add up to much, it's true. I remember the first time I thought that: it was when Domenico Scarpa, on the occasion of the centenary of Levi's birth, pointed out that Levi's complete works comprise some 4,300 pages. It was October 2019, three months after I had received Lorenzo's file from Yad Vashem and realised that it was possible to attempt a biography of Lorenzo. Scarpa said to me that we know almost everything about Levi, but almost nothing about Lorenzo. I hope this is no longer the case. At the time, I thought there were more gaps than there have in fact proved to be, but I already had the feeling that the material I was starting to have in my possession was enough to make it worth a try. The question remains as to why the Yad Vashem procedure was not initiated between 1963 and 1987, the year of Levi's death, or in the years that preceded Carole Angier's stubborn initiative, which began in 1995 and – supported as it was by the Perrone family, Bianca Guidetti Serra, Jean Samuel and Renzo Levi – came to fruition, as we have seen, in 1998.

Lorenzo's surname – whether with one or two 'r's – does not appear to have emerged publicly before the 1960s, through Levi's efforts not before the 1970s, and in his writings not before the 1980s. The first occurrence I have discovered is in the 1963 article in the newspaper *Il Popolo Fossanese*, celebrating the presence in the city of Levi, who had become famous thanks to *The Truce*. The second mention of the surname is in an article in *Famiglia Cristiana* three years later presenting Levi's works. The third was by the woman whom Angier herself considers Levi's 'first biographer', Fiora Vincenti, who included Lorenzo's surname in her book *Invito alla lettura di Primo Levi*, published in 1973 with the author's approval. These are foundational documents, but they do not throw much light on Lorenzo's life and acts. In an article originally entitled '*Nomi and leggende dello scoiattolo*' (published in *La Stampa* in 1980) Levi revealed Lorenzo's surname for the first time in his own writing, but it was only years later, in the interview with Bocca in 1985 – the year when *Other People's Trades* appeared, including the story called 'The Squirrel' – that it would be clear that he was talking about the man who saved him. By the time the clues had become proof, Levi was in a spiral of depression, one 'stupid crisis' after another. 'Last Christmas of the War' is dated 27 March 1984 and, although a private edition was published in Lugano that same year, it would not be made public until December 1986, four months before Levi's suicide. In this story, Levi gives a detailed account of the episode of the package he received from his mother through the chain whose 'last link' was 'Lorenzo Perrone'. It is the only time he writes the surname, apart from in 'The

Squirrel'. He also mentions that he talks about him in *If This Is A Man* and in 'Lorenzo's Return' and describes his death as 'heartbreaking'.

As regards Lorenzo's face: the image showing him in the days when he had been a *bersagliere* had probably been on display since the 1970s – perhaps even since the 1950s, since his first burial; I have no way of knowing – in the cemetery in Fossano. But it was there for private reasons. As far as I know, it was made public thanks to Mayor Manfredi in 1992 and 1993, though circulated only within his community. With the awarding of the title of 'Righteous Among the Nations' in 1998, and then with the publication of the two English-language biographies of Levi in 2002, photographs of Lorenzo would circulate increasingly widely, and now anyone can find them online. In his book, Manfredi mentioned foreign journalists and documentary filmmakers he believed were investigating Lorenzo in order, respectively, to write a book and make a film, but as far as I know no work devoted to him appeared in the following thirty years.

It would have been highly unlikely, in the absence of a surname and, above all, of easily available photographs, for other former slave labourers who had made inquiries to 'recognise' Lorenzo. By now the last survivors are approaching the age of a hundred, if they have not already passed it. I tried in various ways, cross-referencing the data in my possession and groping in the dark, to trace the other men Lorenzo saved. I finally tracked down just one fictional testimony. It was produced by a class of schoolchildren and imagined someone else saved by Lorenzo coming forward to write a letter to a newspaper in which the writer remembered the 'modesty that only good souls are able to have' in order to admonish 'all those who weren't there and those who were and "didn't notice" what was happening in those years', and 'not to forget the man who gave us a little hope with his inner strength: Lorenzo Perrone.' But it is fiction. I can say practically for certain that we will never know who the other people helped by Lorenzo were. As he himself said, 'we're in the world to do good, not to boast.'

...

The house in Via Michelini where Lorenzo spent much of his life no longer exists. It was demolished and rebuilt – 'it was in a pitiful state,'[1] I am told by the architect Claudio Mana, who was in charge of the work. The same thing happened to the barracks, which cast a shadow over the area locals stubbornly refuse to consider a piazza, although it certainly looks like one now. The architect Silvio Pagliero, who was born in 1955 in the house opposite the Perrones' and wrote a graduation thesis on the *Burgué*, makes me smile, telling me that, back in the 1960s, whenever a football ended up in the Perrones' house, it would come back cut to pieces.[2] This, apparently, was the work of the proud Caterina, known as 'Nina', who was still unmarried.

Today, the piazza that stands where Lorenzo and his brothers lived, over which wave the banners of the Borgo Vecchio with its symbol of two fish, is named after the writer and partisan Beppe Fenoglio. In 1997, thanks to Mayor Manfredi, a monument to the migrant was erected there, with a poetic inscription the beginning of which can't help but remind us of Lorenzo ('The wheel of history grinds on' / The toil of the workers grinds on'). In June 2021, a few metres from where Lorenzo lived, a plaque was put up in honour of the 'brave Garibaldian' Giuseppe Valle, who took part in the Expedition of the Thousand at the age of only fourteen, almost a century before Lorenzo was born. Even the building that housed the 'Pigher' has been cleaned up, like many of the buildings in the historic *Burgué*. The firm that took Lorenzo to Buna and the one that was the last to hire him both closed down decades ago, and the tuberculosis ward where he died, situated where the reception desk is now, was demolished in 1970, before the same fate overtook the house in Via Michelini.

The Perrone family home in Via Michelini before its demolition, 1980s.

As for Buna, practically nothing remains of it today. As early as 1947 the survivors of Auschwitz decided to turn Auschwitz I and Auschwitz II-Birkenau into a museum, leaving the other areas of that vast region – the almost fifty sub-camps, the warehouses of the German businesses, and the Monowitz camp itself – to their fate. There remain two monuments and a chemical products factory – yes, that's right: immediately renamed Zakłady Chemiczne, by the beginning of the 2000s it was the largest synthetic rubber factory in Europe – and nothing else. Where Monowitz stood there are now houses.

Physical traces of our passage on this earth fade and vanish. In his book *Epitaph*, the director of the Auschwitz-Birkenau Museum, Piotr Cywiński, referring to proposals for a memorial website to show the place as it was, writes that 'nothing has a more disastrous effect than the passing of time.' I ask Cywiński why he thinks so little has been said about Lorenzo in the seventy years since he abandoned the world, despite the dozens of pages, the hundreds of lines, the thousands of words written and spoken about him by the man who may be the greatest witness of the twentieth century. I tell him that in my opinion he was, in his way, the 'last' of the Just because he was a poor wretch, because he was 'Il Tacca', because he was Lorenzo and not a man in uniform, a diplomat, an industrialist, a person with a good 'position'; but that at least, thanks to Levi, his life story has remained in the light.

Cywiński, aware of the unique importance of concrete gestures, replies that 'memory is a little like our history, built on a narrative full of symbolic characters, and desperately empty of those who have not attained that imaginary pantheon.' He agrees with me, though: 'Primo Levi did right to tell us about Lorenzo, making him part of the story of the Holocaust that will never again remain unknown, anonymous, forgotten.' Perhaps, I say, it's only right that he should finally enter that pantheon. But Cywiński insists on putting side by side with these reflections of his a searing, inescapable image: hundreds of thousands of people deported to Auschwitz are condemned, by contrast, to perennial anonymity, all that remains of them is 'a shoe, a key, a spoon or a suitcase. Or even less. Sometimes, only a transport number.' 'The memory of the Holocaust,' Cywiński remarks, 'is a constant scream and at the same time a heavy silence. And so it must remain for ever.'[3] There should have been hundreds of thousands of 'Lorenzos' so as to leave no room for this scream and this silence, but there weren't. This is another reason why his story, so concrete and so symbolic, should resonate. It is a perennial warning.

I think again of the tears I saw in the eyes of the director Antonio Martorello when I showed him Lorenzo's letters to his friend Primo, the ones written after his homecoming which suddenly emerged in 2022, and I am reminded of what Saleri had told me a few months earlier: 'Lorenzo is the good that exists, the good that exists but doesn't win.'[4] That's what makes the story I have tried to tell so heartrending and the 'message' I glimpse in this life and in this death so terribly human. 'A society that does not see suffering is a society in great danger,' says Jan Brokken after I tell him about Lorenzo. 'Having saved a life is the same as saving the whole world.'[5]

David Grossman says much the same in a moving article about Lorenzo, who on seeing Prisoner 174,517 'refused to ignore his humanity, to collaborate with those who wanted to erase it and, in so doing, saved his life, nothing less. How simple and great was his conduct,' how immense 'his heroic rebellion against the machine of extermination and annihilation' that, looking at Levi 'as one looks at a man' he was able to overturn 'the nature of the situation in which they found themselves.'[6] 'Life stories like Lorenzo's have transformed history, and the way of making it,'[7] as Cesare Bermani said to me. I also asked Thomson and Angier what they remember, what Lorenzo has left behind in the hearts and minds of those who have devoted decades of their lives to Levi. Thomson, who returned to the story of Lorenzo on Holocaust Memorial Day 2022, in a moving article that appeared in *The Tablet*, entitled *The Writer and the Bricklayer: How Primo Levi Survived Auschwitz*, in which he states that there are people in Fossano today who would like to see Lorenzo canonised, replies like this: 'on the one hand, Lorenzo was the providential figure who made it possible for Primo Levi to survive the camp and therefore to bear witness and write what is one of the cornerstones of twentieth-century culture;'[8] on the other, he is the extreme representative of what in the Anglo-Saxon world is depicted as 'peasant culture' a 'way of looking at the world' perhaps typical of the lower classes, endowed with a solid 'morality'. He, who knew perfectly well what it means to be 'the last', is elevated to the archetype of a 'peasant' world that has now almost disappeared, a kind of vanished figure of that reality with its codes and values.

This reminds me of what was said to me – exactly two years after we first met – by Luca Bedino, spokesman for the Archives of Fossano, who has followed every step of this attempt to write a biography: Lorenzo's goodness wasn't culturally constructed, but 'genuine, spontaneous, immediate.'[9] That reminds me of Don Lenta: Thomson tells me that, of course, he was referring to him when talking in his article about those who wished to canonise Lorenzo. The religious dimension of Lorenzo's story is very strong, Thomson insists, and it seems to me that it brings the life of this man full circle: an unbeliever but one who was christened and given the last rites, a man buried in a civil ceremony – which perhaps extended inside the church of San Giorgio – but in a hushed silence in which his friend's sense of the sacred – that friend also an atheist – rang out loud and clear. I also see tears in the white sweater Levi wore and the few words he spoke: he was one of those men who, although 'hardened' and hiding his face, was not afraid to cry. Perhaps in this way Lorenzo saved him one last time. And now it can be said, from a strictly Levian, secular and non-religious viewpoint: Primo Levi rarely used the word 'saint' – insisting most of the time on the ambiguity of human conduct, but Lorenzo was, as we have seen, among the very few real people to whom he did not hesitate to apply the word. Is this, then, the kernel of his discourse on each and every one of us, an immaculate counterbalance – although Levi [10] – to the 'greyness' that constantly infects us?

'Words may be poor things, but they remain,' Angier wrote twenty years ago in her biography of Levi. 'It may be a hopeless task to make a man live again on the page, but it is the only place where he can live again at all.'[11] I asked Angier, thanks to whom this research has been possible, to return to the wonderful image of the 'centrepiece' of her investigation of the man she herself described as 'a researcher, a student of humanity'[12] who spent all his life searching for an answer to the question, 'what is a man?' And she confirms to me this feeling of mine, on which I have insisted in these pages but that I had perhaps never managed to develop this far: 'Lorenzo is crucial' for understanding Primo Levi and his *search*, she says. Because, as we know, Levi 'searched for humanity in ordinary people and among them he found the deepest humanity.' Not many people came out of that place without losing themselves, as Angier reminds me. Even if we scrape away the epic patina his friend Primo gave him, there is little to add: that is how Lorenzo was. Finally, and fundamentally – and it is here that Angier gets to the crux of the matter, and I fully agree with her – what Levi says of him answers the question he asked all his life, because it can be condensed into this statement: 'This is a man.'

...

Was I still missing something, on the factual level, about Lorenzo's life? Of course I was, that's only natural. It took me far too long to realise that history is like that.

When I was still a child and went to the cinema with my father to see *The Truce*, Angier and Thomson were already scouring Fossano and its surroundings in search of testimonies about Lorenzo, saving, developing and preserving them. But since then, time has carried away the vast majority of the witnesses, both known to me and unknown, including Mayor Manfredi, who died in 2005. Lorenzo's nephew Beppe responded magnificently to my questions in 2020 – and so did his little niece Emma, whom I met in the summer of 2022 to tell her that the book was finally done. Emma, who has lovingly preserved the parchment from Yad Vashem, gifted me perhaps the most beautiful image of all – I had difficulty holding back my tears. She was almost seven when he came home and still only fourteen when Lorenzo died, and she remembers him as 'perhaps the most handsome' of her uncles. She tells me about the times when 'all you could see were four legs, my two little ones and his', because Lorenzo would take her with him to the tavern, surely the 'Pigher', hiding her under his cape, and order a lemonade for her and a glass of dark wine for himself. And then Grandma Giovanna or her aunt Nina, who brought her up in the *Burgué*, would come looking for her, because that wasn't a place suitable for a little girl. But she loved her uncle, and he loved her, and I know that when they could they went there again on the sly, and God alone knows know what they said to each other, 'Il Tacca' and little Emma, who is now an eighty-five-year-old with bright eyes and a proud demeanour. 'Unforgettable,'[13] is how she describes her uncle.

...

It is now more than seventy years since Lorenzo died, and well over a century since his birth. On the occasion of the centenary of Levi's birth, in 2019, I attended various events, looking in the speeches about the chemist, witness and writer, for traces of 'his friend Lorenzo'. I also saw his children Renzo and Lisa Lorenza but didn't dare say anything to them. I know, though, what Levi's second child, named after Lorenzo, said on the occasion of the conferring of the title of 'Righteous Among the Nations', exactly twenty years earlier:

> Nobody deserved this recognition more than him, because at risk to his life and of grave personal loss he helped our dear father and many others to survive. Perhaps he would have greeted this ceremony with his sad smile, convinced that what he had done was simply his duty: a lonely and profoundly good man marked for death by that terrible experience.

Lorenzo hadn't helped only Primo: this is a huge legacy. The question isn't only, how many other people did Lorenzo help? It's also, how many 'Lorenzos' were there about whom we know nothing? How many bricklayers on the margins of 'Suiss' were crucial to the survival of prisoners, whether a lot or a few? And the final question – although there is never an end to our search for meaning – is: if everyone had been like

Lorenzo, could a place like Auschwitz have even existed?

'It would be wonderful to tell the story of the "Lorenzos"', we read in the newspaper *Il Popolo Fossanese*, reporting a presentation in Fossano of *If This Is A Man*, but such people being 'good and timid, little is known of them.' As far as I'm aware – and here I'm grateful to the invaluable groundwork of Angier and Thomson – this article by Domenico Romita, a long-standing teacher at the local high school, is the first public mention of Lorenzo in the Fossano press. For two decades, it will also be the only one. But it's already quite something, considering that the issue is dated 15 June 1963, soon after the publication of *The Truce*. Admittedly, Lorenzo had been dead for some time, but this was recent history, and it opened up a past that was still alive.

It can't be taken for granted that the past is able to live. All too often, past events become scattered by time and are only rescued from oblivion thanks to a miraculous combination of circumstances. Lorenzo is at least in part a celebrity today in Fossano (a city which can boast other stories of the Righteous, like that of Don Antonio Mana, Maria Angelica Ferrari, Mother Superior of the Dominican Institute, and the Grasso family, from the district of Loreto). In the sixty years since that first article, a great deal has happened. In 1982 Don Lenta, the former parish priest of Fossano, proudly claimed that 'in the evocative pages of the latest collection by the well-known writer' (*Moments of Reprieve*), there was 'a bricklayer from the Old Quarter of Fossano' about whom Levi had at last felt free to speak, 'released from the discretion' that had stopped him previously. 'Lorenzo's Return' was the only story in the collection that had not appeared before.

In the early 1980s, then, awareness increased. (In 1993,

five years before Lorenzo became a 'Righteous Among the Nations', Mayor Giuseppe Manfredi devoted a four-page eulogy to him in his imposing two-volume history of Fossano during the twentieth century. Thanks to the patient work of certain individuals and community groups, Lorenzo is definitely a figure in the city's pantheon today. 'But he became that only recently,' I am told by Luisa Mellano, president of the Fossano branch of the National Association of Italian Partisans. According to the librarian Carlo Morra, now in his eighties, who met Lorenzo as a child and who was interviewed by Samuele Saleri, the author of the only existing work on Lorenzo – a masterly (unpublished) graduation thesis from the academic year 2017/18 – most inhabitants of Fossano these days don't have any idea who he was. Even members of his family didn't know or didn't see the value of his engagement with Levi for a long time. His family even told Angier that for forty years they were ashamed of Lorenzo; 'because that is how heroism can be – especially the best, unrewarded kind: a historical glory but a personal burden, not only for the hero, and not only at the time.'

In April 2015, near the school in Fossano named after Levi, a small olive tree from Jerusalem was planted 'in memory of the bond between Primo Levi and Lorenzo Perone' – the surname written with a single 'r'. At about the same time, on the occasion of the seventieth anniversary of the country's liberation from Fascist rule, a celebratory local publication saw the light of day. The first section, *I fossanesi e la guerra*, opens with a brief portrait of Lorenzo. The author, Guillermo Vincenti, uses Primo Levi's writings, documentation from Yad Vashem, obtained through Levi's son Renzo, and the only remaining official trace of Lorenzo in Fossano: a plaque unveiled in Viale delle Alpi in 25 April 2004, as sources. The plaque, realised with the passionate collaboration of the local librarian, Giovanni Menardi, reads:

To Lorenzo Perone (1904–1952)

>Along this avenue you often walked
>Lorenzo Perone from Fossano
>You were a son of the Borgo Vecchio
>a bricklayer of few words
>In 1944 in the Buna-Werke factory
>adjacent to Auschwitz extermination camp
>you saved the soul and body of Primo Levi
>with your bread giving him hope
>at the risk of your own life this is why you were honoured
>in Israel with the title of 'Righteous Among the Nations'
>You were a humble and generous son of Fossano
>   (B.M.)

It is 'a fitting even though belated "revelation"' as Menardi would declare to Saleri, recalling his contacts with a Dutch director, Yvonne Scholten, who wanted to make a film about Levi, and with Carole Angier while she was working on her meticulous biography. If it weren't for the inexhaustible mine of Levi's own works, writing about Lorenzo would be a guaranteed failure, especially as far what happened in and around the Lager is concerned. The documentation in the file for the procedure undertaken by Yad Vashem in November 1995, at Angier's urging, to name Lorenzo as a 'Righteous Among the Nations' – 115 pages –

remains crucial and irreplaceable. Thanks to these diligent records it is possible to restore three dimensions to a man the memory of whom might, in other circumstances, have simply disappeared.

As Patrick Modiano reminds us in *Dora Bruder*, a stubborn attempt (only partly successful as research but of great literary value) to rescue the story of a Holocaust victim from oblivion, the world is crowded with 'people – dead or alive – to be registered in the category of "unidentified individuals."' Grappling with the task of writing about Lorenzo, the man who made 'the first substantial contribution to the survival of the young Piedmontese graduate' without a solid documentary foundation would be a long, futile struggle. Or else it would prove to be little more than a learned *divertissement*, along the lines of what the French historian Alain Corbin tried to do (just about getting away with it) in his *The Life of an Unknown: The Rediscovered World of a Clockmaker in Nineteenth-Century France*, tacking the challenge of writing the biography of a Mr Nobody, a clog maker literally chosen at random in an archive.

Taking as his starting point the vast gaps in our knowledge of the ancient world, Bertolt Brecht asked in his famous poem 'Questions From a Worker Who Reads': 'who built Thebes of the seven gates? [...] Where, the evening that the Great Wall of China was finished, did the masons go?' In the case of the clog maker Louis-François Pinagot, who fell into total oblivion and was 'resuscitated' by Corbin, the latter described his work not as an 'impossible' biography, but an 'evocation,' a 'fleeting resurrection' of a man who had until then been 'swallowed up' by history, 'without any possibility of leaving a trace of himself in the memory of men.' Quite another fate has befallen Lorenzo. That's because he was lucky enough not only to be born in the following century – Pinagot died on 31 January 1876, Lorenzo was born twenty-eight years later – but also, as we have seen, to cross the path of a future star, who would recall fragments of his life story, actions and words.

'It would be wonderful,' said the first article about Lorenzo half a century ago – it would be useful and necessary, I add – to tell their story, the story of the last of the Just, the last who became first and did not take advantage. It would be vital, and we should do so every day. Because Lorenzo built something immense: faith in humanity.

> Do not be afraid if the work is hard:
> you who are less tired are needed.
> Since your senses are fine-tuned, you hear
> how hollow sounds the earth beneath your feet.
> Think again about our mistakes:
> there have even been those among us
> who have set off on a blind search
> like a blindfolded man repeating an outline,
> and have set sail like privateers,
> and have tried with goodwill.
> Help, you who are unsure.
> Try, although you are unsure,
> because you are unsure. [...]
> Do not be dismayed by the debris
> or by the stench of the garbage: we
> cleared it with our bare hands
> in the years when we were your age.
> Keep going, as best you can. [...]
>   — Primo Levi, 'Mandate,' 24 June 1986

ACKNOWLEDGEMENTS

As in all my books, behind this one there is, let me stress, a huge amount of teamwork, spread over several years of conception, study, research and writing – although, obviously, the responsibility for these pages remains exclusively mine. There was a time when I considered that this would be an (almost) 'impossible' biography, but the support that so many people have given my research, especially in its accelerated finale, has made it possible for me to trace a surprising amount of material. Confronting the life and works of Primo Levi, the supporting actor of this story, has been stimulating, and has necessitated a dialogue on tiptoe with those who have investigated his life story, his texts and the documentation he bequeathed to us in these last few decades. There are many people to thank, and I shall try to do so by following the thread of this biography, a biography that was difficult at first but proved to be gradually more feasible and has, I hope, finally succeeded in giving Lorenzo his full three dimensions.

First and foremost, I am infinitely grateful to Lorenzo's nephew Beppe Perone (with one 'r') – who sadly died on 3 March 2023 – and niece Emma Bard née Barberis (thank you, Jamie!) the daughter of Giovanna. In Fossano and Turin respectively, they gave me their time and allowed me to 'see' their uncle through their eyes. As regards the relationship between Lorenzo and Primo, the pillar of this book and of both men's lives, my first thank you goes to Liad Mousan Shemesh, Coordinator of Public Affairs and Research of the Righteous Among the Nations Department. My contact with those who over the past few decades have studied Levi, told his story and preserved his vast cultural and human legacy has been fundamental to this book; I postponed that contact until I was approaching the end of the first draft, but it proved crucial. So thank you to Carole Angier and Ian Thomson, who in the summer of 2022 both went back to their work of twenty years earlier and placed at my total disposal their memories and the sources they uncovered at the time, over and above what is in their books. Thank you to both of them also for their extensive feedback during the course of my work and for the valuable interviews that greatly enrich, I think, the last pages of this book. A huge thank you to the Primo Levi International Study Centre, represented by its president Fabio Levi, its director Daniela Muraca and Cristina Zuccaro, who was in charge of the archives and the bibliographical heritage. As well as revealing to me the existence of Lorenzo's letters and postcards, and the unexpected donation of the Angier Archive, they put at my total disposal their bibliographical and audio-visual collections beyond the published work of Primo Levi, and listened to my doubts and obsessions, helping me to hone the text down to its smallest details. Thank you to the archivists and writers, thinkers and historians who have kept the records to enable this work. Several of the chapter titles, including Chapter 3, 'And Night Came,' Chapter 10, 'Us Few Still Alive' and Chapter 12, 'And They Will Pay Back' are quotes from Levi's works. The credit for the title 'The Story of the Holy Drinker' for Chapter 13 belongs to Ian Thomson, taking Joseph Roth's *The Legend of the Holy Drinker* as inspiration. Thank you to Domenico Scarpa for commenting on these pages once the first draft had been finished, helping me in particular to smooth over a false note; in addition, his outstanding latest work (*Bibliografia di Primo Levi ovvero Il primo Atlante*, Einaudi / Primo Levi International Study Centre, 2022), was of

ACKNOWLEDGEMENTS

enormous help to me in completing the final confirmations and the work on the endnotes (in particular as regards the identification of the first appearances of Levi's' writings, before these were published in volume form). A huge thank you to Marco Belpoliti, editor of Levi's works and author of *Primo Levi: An Identikit* (Seagull, 2022) for encouraging me and discussing with me in the course of my work some of the most serious and playful matters treated in this book – like suicide and wine, respectively – and for his truly moving feedback. Thank you also to Alberto Cavaglion, among other things editor of the annotated edition of *If This Is A Man*, for doing the same, with his usual honesty and affection. Thank you to Martina Mengoni and thank you to Howard Falksohn and Sonia Bacca of the Wiener Holocaust Library in London for combing through the Ian Thomson Collection in search of information about Lorenzo.

In Fossano, Luca Bedino was much more than a passionate and meticulous archivist: he was a guide. As well as locating everything there is about Lorenzo in the register office – from the birth of his father to his own death certificate – he accompanied me to the cemetery on the trail of Lorenzo's two burial places. On 1 May 2024, between the release of the Italian and English editions of this book, Luca passed by. I remember him with brotherly love and infinite gratitude. Thank you also to Massimo Nardi, general secretary of the municipality. A huge thank you to Michele Tavella, long-time inhabitant of the *Burgué*, who placed at my total disposal his social and visual knowledge and along with Caterina Rossi also sifted through this text with me to root out any dialect errors. Thanks to Silvio Pagliero, who together with Michele helped me to reconstruct the topography of the Old Town, in addition to providing valuable photographs. Thank you to Antonio Martorello and his deep humanity, thank you to Luisa Mellano, president of the Fossano branch of the National Association of Italian Partisans – and to Fabrizio Biolè – thank you to Pinuccio Bellone and Agnese Fissore who were the first to open the doors of the city to me, thank you to Cecilia Di Marco and Adelina Brizio for talking to me and a big thank you to Samuele Saleri – from Brescia, like Alberto Dalla Volta, but I'm sure he'll forgive me if I include him among those born or adopted in Fossano – for having been the first to write about Lorenzo in his fascinating graduation thesis. Thank you to the architect Claudio Mana for the details about the demolition of the house in Via Michelini.

As regards the 'Granda', the province of Cuneo, my most heartfelt thank you goes to the friends of the D.L. Bianco Historical Institute of the Resistance and Contemporary Society in the Province of Cuneo and in particular to the director Gigi Garelli, to Alessandra Demichelis who is widely quoted here; thank you also to Chiara Zangola of the state archives in Cuneo for attempting the (im)possible enterprise of tracking down a certain kind of information.

Finding traces of the firm of Beotti proved fruitful thanks to the well-known contract preserved in the Alessandrina University Library in Rome (thank you Valentina Corridori) and thank you to the state archive of Piacenza (thank you Arianna Bonè) and to the Chamber of Commerce of Piacenza (thank you Lucia Casella). A heartfelt thank you also to Marta Rutigliano and Ippolito Negri for making it possible for me to 'join the dots' to Antonio Camuso of the Benedetto Petrone Historical Archive for our discussion. Thank you of course to Cesare Bermani for the irreplaceable work done by him decades ago and for the wonderful day we spent together, talking about Lorenzo and about how one should try to tell a story.

ACKNOWLEDGEMENTS

I have felt at home at the Auschwitz-Birkenau Memorial and Museum for a dozen years. To complete this research I once again disturbed people I already knew and others who placed their competence at my disposal for archival, historical and biographical details. Thank you above all to the director, Piotr M.A. Cywiński, for his humanity and his great helpfulness, thank you Michele Andreola, an irreplaceable guide (in both a narrow and a broad sense); Elżbieta Cajzer, Head of Auschwitz Museum Collections, for that first discussion and groundwork way back in 2015; thank you Dagmar Kopijasz, founder of the Foundation of Memory Sites near Auschwitz-Birkenau and to Agnieszka Kita; thank you to the archivist Szymon Kowalski and to Piotr Setkiewicz, Head of the Research Center and author of the essential monograph on Monowitz. With regard to the letters sent to Primo's home through his friend Lorenzo, I thank Fabrizio Salmoni, the son of Alberto and Bianca Guidetti Serra, for our discussion.

Coming now to the return journey and the immediate post-War period, I apologise to the dozens of Peruchs in Friuli whom I bothered (and I thank the director of the state archive in Bolzano / Staatsarchive Bozen, Dr Harald Toniatti, as well as apologising to him for the false lead; thank you to Monica Emmanuelli, director of the Friulan Institute for the History of the Liberation Movement in Udine for rooting through its archive and to Luciano Patat for his meticulous investigation) and to the dozens of Duttos who met the same fate: a thank you in particular to Luisella Dutto, and then to Vera Masoero of the Cuneo branch of the Italian General Confederation of Labor of Cuneo, who (with the Confederation's Italian Federation of Woodworkers, Builders and Similar Trades and with Anna Maria Tomatis, Nello Fierro and Ilenia Basso) followed up these leads like a bloodhound; thank you also to

Stefania Cardona of the Chamber of Commerce in Cuneo and a Beppe Segre, head of the Jewish Community of Turin.

In Savigliano, the endpoint of this biography, heartfelt thanks to Silvia Olivero of the City archives, Angela Cacciaguerra of the register office, Cinzia Elena Mario for having introduced me to the memories of the Savigliano health service, and with her Doctor Luciano Galletto, Beatrice and Adriana Fruttero – daughters of Francesco and granddaughters of Enrico – for having shared with me memories and mementoes and to Dr Giovanni Niffeneger for his valuable testimony and moving tenacity.

For the investigation into the medical records, death and funeral of Lorenzo, thank you Susanna and Sara of the Vignolo Archive (Amos Society), thank you to the Archiepiscopal Archive of Turin, to Laura Fiorito of the Parish Archive of the Church of Santa Maria della Pieve in Savigliano, and to Rossella Fiorillo of the Archive of the Diocese of Fossano.

Thanks are also due to those who guided or helped me in my research (my friend and sleuth Leonardo Mineo, with Attilio Offman and Antonio Polosa; Barbara Berruti, Chiara Colombini, Andrea D'Arrigo, Tobia Imperato and Cristina Sara of the Giorgio Agosti Piedmont Institute for the History of the Resistance and Contemporary Society; Fabio Cancelliere of the National Cinematographic Archive of the Resistance; Andrea Spagnolo; Anna Stefi; Marta Margotti; Gadi Luzzatto Voghera and Laura Brazzo of the Centre of Jewish Contemporary Documentation; Martina Landi of 'Gariwo, the forest of the Just'; Mirna Campanella and Luisa Alonzi from the Library of the Diocese of Frosinone), in my reflections that made the writing possible and in the discussions we had in the course of the work (David Bidussa, Fausto Ciuffi, Phil Cooke, Enrico Deaglio, Giovanni De Luna, Francesco

ACKNOWLEDGEMENTS

Filippi, Eric Gobetti, Wlodek Goldkorn, Wolf Gruner, Bruno Maida, Enrico Manera, Martina Merletti, Marco Ponti with 'his' Hermes, Alice Ravinale and Edoardo Morino, Tommaso Speccher and Gabriel Eikenberg) and to those who represent the architrave of the civil debate and commitment which is the first premise of this work: the Deina Association, which I had the honour of co-founding, and with which I went countless times to Auschwitz and other memorials all over Europe; thank you in particular to Elena Bissaca, Francesca Poli and Davide Toso, who may remember the first glimmer of this adventure and to Ruben Bianchetti and Daniele Regoli for always being there.

Last but not least, thank you to Carlo Ballero and Anna Mondino for helping me to set the fire. Thank you to Silvia, Ada and Alberto of the Meucci Agency for guiding me every step of the way and thank you – today more than ever – to Giovanni Carletti, editor and friend, who together with Carolina Coriani, Agnese Gualdrini, Giovanna Mollica, Nicoletta Cavalluzzi and Stefano Savella was able to turn the typescript into a book. Thank you to Alessandro, Giuseppe, Antonia and Bianca Laterza for believing in every project of ours with conviction and passion; to Elizabeth Briggs and all The Westbourne Press team for this wonderful edition (and for the passion and enthusiasm with which they embraced this adventure), and to Howard Curtis for the excellent translation for the English-speaking world. My final thanks to my great family, in particular to my mother and father, excellent readers of so many of my things and who read *Un uomo di poche parole* with special care; and to Laura, Lorenzo and Tommaso, because they have taught me what loving means.

NOTES

PROLOGUE

1. *Il Coraggio e la pietà. Gli ebrei e l'Italia durante la guerra 1940–5* directed by Nicola Caracciolo, Italy 1986.
2. *La guerra agli ebrei 1943–1945* by Liliana Picciotto, p. 70 from *Storia e Memoria* of the Istituto ligure per la storia della Resistenza e dell'età contemporanea (ILSREC), no. 2/2014.
3. *If This Is A Man*; 'Lorenzo's Return' in *Moments of Reprieve* by Primo Levi.
4. For example, Alvin Rosenfeld, 'Questions and Answers at Indiana University', in *Midstream, A Monthly Jewish Review*, XXXII, April 1986, No. 4.
5. *Il Giudice dei Giusti*, by Emanuela Audisio and Gabriele Nissim (2013).
6. 'The Righteous Among the Nations', 'Names of Righteous by Country Statistics' (accessed on 1 January 2021). By 2021, this number had risen to 27,921 total 'Righteous' and 744 Italian 'Righteous'.
7. *If This Is A Man* by Primo Levi.
8. *The Drowned and the Saved* by Primo Levi.
9. *If This Is A Man* by Primo Levi.
10. Especially letter by Carole Angier, 6 November 1995, to Mordecai Paldiel, 23 January 1996, to id., 18 April 1996, Yad Vashem Archive.
11. 'The Mark of the Chemist' in *Other People's Trades* by Primo Levi.
12. 'Vanidium' in *The Periodic Table* by Primo Levi.

CHAPTER 1: TACCA FROM THE BURGUÉ

1. *The Drowned and the Saved* by Primo Levi.
2. 'Lorenzo's Return' in *Moments of Reprieve* by Primo Levi.
3. Ibid.
4. *If This Is A Man* by Primo Levi.
5. Ibid.
6. 'Iron' in *The Periodic Table* by Primo Levi.
7. *If This Is A Man* by Primo Levi.
8. 'Lorenzo's Return' in *Moments of Reprieve* by Primo Levi.

9 *The Drowned and the Saved* by Primo Levi.
10 'Lorenzo's Return' in *Moments of Reprieve* by Primo Levi.
11 'Vanadium' in *The Periodic Table* by Primo Levi.
12 *Il Coraggio e la pietà* by Nicola Caracciolo.
13 'Lorenzo's Return' in *Moments of Reprieve* by Primo Levi.
14 Giuseppe Perone to the author, 29 January 2020.
15 According to Levi's biographer Carole Angier, who interviewed three of Lorenzo's relatives, including Beppe, around 1975.
16 Giuseppe Perone to Carlo Greppi, 29 January 2020.
17 Michele Tavella to Carlo Greppi, 29 January 2020.
18 Giuseppe Perone to Carlo Greppi, 29 January 2020.
19 Michele Tavella to Carlo Greppi, 29 January 2020; see also *The Double Bond* by Carole Angier (Viking, London 2002); *Primo Levi: A Life* by Ian Thomson (Henry Holt, 2014).
20 Michele Tavella to Carlo Greppi, 29 January 2020.
21 *The Double Bond* by Carole Angier p. 321.
22 *Ibid*, p.321.
23 Luisa Mellano to Carlo Greppi, 21 April 2022.
24 Giuseppe Perone to Carlo Greppi, 29 January 2020.
25 As a peasant says in Nuto Revelli's *Il Mondo dei vinti*.
26 *Primo Levi: A Life* by Ian Thomson.
27 *Ibid*.

CHAPTER 2: KNIVES AND CURSES

1 *Il Fossanese*, Saturday 7 September 1918.
2 *Il Cielo sopra il castello* by Beppe Manfredi (Fossano, 1993) pp. 93–4.
3 *Memorie di un barbiere* by Giovanni Germanetto (Rome, 1945,) *passim*; *Cuneo, le loro prigioni* by Livio Berardo (Turin, 1994) p. 8.
4 *Il buon tempo antico'. Cronache criminali dalle campagne cuneesi nel Novecento* in *'Per un fazzoletto di terra'. Studi sul mondo rurale cuneese nel Novecento* by Alessandra Demichelis, 'Il Presente e la Storia' No. 95 June 2019, p. 119.
5 *Ibid*, p. 98.
6 *Ibid*, p. 105.
7 *Ibid*, p. 114.
8 *Il Lessico dialettale del lavoro contadino nel* Mondo dei Vinti *di Nuto Revelli* by Gianluca Cinelli, p. 67.
9 The first of these epithets probably just means 'hard man', the second may, hypothetically, mean 'pig' in local dialect.
10 'Il buon tempo antico' by Alessandra Demichelis, pp. 116–7.

11 *Al lavoro nella Germania di Hitler* by Cesare Bermani (Turin 1998) p. 53 and p. 29.
12 'Lorenzo's Return' in *Moments of Reprieve.* by Primo Levi.
13 *Cuneo. Da serbatoio di manodopera per l'estero a provincia affluente* by Renata Allio in Rapport italiani nel mondo 2020, Rome 2006, pp. 206–8.
14 *Les Javanais* by Jean Malaquais (Denoël, 1939).
15 *L'Invasion* by Louis Bertrand (Nelson, 1911).
16 *Cuneo. Da serbatoio di manodopera per l'estero a provincia affluente* by Renata Allio, p. 212.

CHAPTER 3: AND NIGHT CAME

1 *Al lavoro nella Germania di Hitler* by Cesare Bermani, pp. 23–5.
2 *Ibid*, pp. 57-8.
3 'Lorenzo's Return' in *Moments of Reprieve* by Primo Levi.
4 *Ibid*.
5 *The Drowned and the Saved* by Primo Levi.
6 *Primo Levi: A Life* by Ian Thomson.
7 'Fine Settimana' by Primo Levi.
8 'Il Versificatore' by Primo Levi.
9 *The Wrench* by Primo Levi.
10 *If This Is A Man* by Primo Levi.
11 *The Wrench* by Primo Levi.
12 *The Periodic Table* by Primo Levi.
13 'The Death of Marinese' in *A Tranquil Star* by Primo Levi.
14 *The Periodic Table* by Primo Levi.
15 *If This Is A Man* by Primo Levi.
16 *The Periodic Table* by Primo Levi.
17 *If This Is A Man* by Primo Levi.
18 *Ibid*.
19 *Ibid*.
20 *Ibid*.
21 *Ibid*.
22 *Ibid*.
23 *If Not Now, When?* by Primo Levi.
24 *Ibid*.
25 *The Wrench* by Primo Levi.

NOTES

CHAPTER 4: WASTING AWAY

1. *If This Is A Man* by Primo Levi.
2. Ibid.
3. Primo Levi in an interview for TV programme *Sorgente di life* in 1983.
4. *The Drowned and the Saved* by Primo Levi.
5. 'Translating Kafka' in *The Mirror Maker* by Primo Levi.

CHAPTER 5: THE LANGUAGE OF SURVIVAL

1. *In the Shadow of Death* by Gordon J. Horwitz (Free Press, 1990) p. 3.
2. *The Drowned and the Saved* by Primo Levi.
3. 'Lorenzo's Return' in *Moments of Reprieve* by Primo Levi.
4. From a 1974 interview, quoted in *Primo Levi: A Life*.
5. 'Lorenzo's Return' in *Moments of Reprieve* by Primo Levi, quoted by Ian Thomson.
6. Ibid.
7. *If This Is A Man* by Primo Levi.
8. Ibid.
9. Ibid.
10. Ibid.
11. Emma Barberis to Carlo Greppi, 9 September 2022.
12. Giuseppe Perone to Carlo Greppi, 29 January 2020.
13. *If Not Now, When?* by Primo Levi.
14. Ibid.
15. *The Drowned and the Saved* by Primo Levi.
16. *The Wrench* by Primo Levi.
17. *If This Is A Man* by Primo Levi.
18. Ibid.
19. Ibid.
20. *The Drowned and the Saved* by Primo Levi.
21. Ibid.

CHAPTER 6: WORKING IN 'SUISS'

1. *If This Is A Man* by Primo Levi.
2. Ibid.
3. Ibid.
4. Ibid.
5. *The Truce* by Primo Levi.

6 *Ibid.*
7 *If This Is A Man* by Primo Levi.
8 Postscript to *If This is A Man* and *The Truce* by Primo Levi.

CHAPTER 7: MESSAGES

1 *Al lavoro nella Germania di Hitler* by Cesare Bermani, pp. 242–52.
2 'Lorenzo's Return' in *Moments of Reprieve* by Primo Levi.
3 *Ibid.*
4 *Ibid.*
5 *Ibid.*
6 *Ibid.*
7 *If This Is A Man* by Primo Levi.
8 *The Drowned and the Saved* by Primo Levi.
9 *Ibid.*
10 'Lorenzo's Return' in *Moments of Reprieve* by Primo Levi.
11 *The Drowned and the Saved* by Primo Levi.
12 *If This Is A Man* by Primo Levi.
13 'Lorenzo's Return' in *Moments of Reprieve* by Primo Levi.
14 *Remembering Survival: Inside a Nazi Slave-Labor Camp* by Christopher R. Browning (W.W. Norton & Co., 2010) p. 298.
15 *If This Is A Man* by Primo Levi.
16 *The Double Bond* by Carole Angier, p. 322.
17 'Vanadium' in *The Periodic Table* by Primo Levi.
18 Quoted in Giorgio Vaccarino, *Nuove fonti sull'imperialismo economico nazista. La IG Farben e il 'nuovo ordine'*, 'Italia contemporanea', December 1987.
19 *If Not Now, When?* by Primo Levi.
20 *Primo Levi: A Life* by Ian Thomson.
21 *The Sixth Day* by Primo Levi.
22 *Primo Levi, l'Amico*, Zamorani by Bianca Guidetti Serra (2012) p. 8.
23 'A Disciple' in *Moments of Reprieve* by Primo Levi.
24 *The Drowned and the Saved* by Primo Levi.
25 *Primo Levi: A Life* by Ian Thomson.
26 *Bianca la rossa* by Bianca Guidetti Serra (Einaudi, 2009) p. 55.
27 *Primo Levi: A Life* by Ian Thomson.
28 'A Disciple' in *Moments of Reprieve* by Primo Levi.
29 *Ibid.*
30 Quoted in *Primo Levi: A Life* by Ian Thomson.
31 *Primo Levi, l'Amico, Zamorani* by Bianca Guidetti Serra.
32 *Primo Levi: A Life* by Ian Thomson.

NOTES

33 *The Drowned and the Saved* by Primo Levi.
34 *Ibid.*
35 *Primo Levi: A Life* by Ian Thomson.
36 *The Sixth Day* by Primo Levi.
37 *If This Is A Man* by Primo Levi.
38 Yad Vashem (@yadvashem) on Twitter, 8 November 2020.
39 *Golden Harvest: Events on the Periphery of the Holocaust* by Jan Tomasz Gross, p. 69.
40 *The Drowned and the Saved* by Primo Levi.
41 'Lorenzo's Return' in *Moments of Reprieve* by Primo Levi.
42 *Ibid.*

CHAPTER 8: THE NIGHT THAT REFUSES TO END

1 'Lorenzo's Return' in *Moments of Reprieve* by Primo Levi.
2 *Ibid.*
3 'Carbon' in *The Periodic Table* by Primo Levi.
4 *Other People's Trades* by Primo Levi.
5 Quoted in *Primo Levi: A Life* by Ian Thomson.
6 'Iron' in *The Periodic Table* by Primo Levi.
7 *Ibid.*
8 'Potassium' in *The Periodic Table* by Primo Levi.
9 'Iron' in *The Periodic Table* by Primo Levi.
10 *Ibid.*
11 'Vanadium' in *The Periodic Table* by Primo Levi.
12 'Last Christmas of the War' in *Moments of Reprieve* by Primo Levi.
13 'Cesare's Last Adventure' in *Moments of Reprieve* by Primo Levi.
14 'Lorenzo's Return' in *Moments of Reprieve* by Primo Levi.
15 *If This Is A Man* by Primo Levi.
16 'Last Christmas of the War' in *Moments of Reprieve* by Primo Levi.
17 *Ibid.*
18 *If This Is A Man* by Primo Levi.
19 'Lorenzo's Return' in *Moments of Reprieve* by Primo Levi.
20 *If This Is A Man* by Primo Levi.
21 *The Double Bond* by Carole Angier, p. 350.
22 'Vanadium' in *The Periodic Table* by Primo Levi.
23 'Lorenzo's Return' in *Moments of Reprieve* by Primo Levi.
24 *Ibid.*

CHAPTER 9: WALKING

1 *The Truce* by Primo Levi.
2 'Lorenzo's Return' in *Moments of Reprieve* by Primo Levi.
3 *Ibid.*
4 *Ibid.*
5 *Ibid.*
6 *If This Is A Man* by Primo Levi.
7 *The Double Bond* by Carole Angier, p. 422.
8 *If This Is A Man* by Primo Levi.
9 *Primo Levi: A Life* by Ian Thomson.
10 *The Double Bond* by Carole Angier, p. 335.
11 'Cerium' in *The Periodic Table* by Primo Levi.
12 *If This Is A Man* by Primo Levi.
13 *Ibid.*
14 *The Double Bond* by Carole Angier, p. 89.
15 *Gli schiavi di Hitler* by Lazzero Ricciotti, (Mondadori, 1996) p. 301.
16 'Lorenzo's Return' in *Moments of Reprieve* by Primo Levi.
17 *Primo Levi: A Life* by Ian Thomson.
18 *The Double Bond* by Carole Angier, p. 422.
19 'Lorenzo's Return' in *Moments of Reprieve* by Primo Levi.
20 *Primo Levi: A Life* by Ian Thomson.
21 'Lorenzo's Return' in *Moments of Reprieve* by Primo Levi.
22 *Ibid.*
23 *The Truce* by Primo Levi.
24 *If This Is A Man* by Primo Levi.

CHAPTER 10: US FEW STILL ALIVE

1 *The Double Bond* by Carole Angier, p. 422.
2 *Ibid*, p. 422.
3 *Ibid*, p. 422–3.
4 *Primo Levi: A Life* by Ian Thomson.
5 *The Double Bond* by Carole Angier, p. 424.
6 *Primo Levi: A Life* by Ian Thomson.
7 'Argon' in *The Periodic Table* by Primo Levi.
8 *Primo Levi: A Life* by Ian Thomson.
9 'Rappoport's Testament' in *Moments of Reprieve* by Primo Levi.
10 *The Double Bond* by Carole Angier, p. 416.
11 *The Truce* by Primo Levi.
12 *The Double Bond* by Carole Angier, p. 416.

NOTES

13 'Nickel' in *The Periodic Table* by Primo Levi.
14 *The Wrench* by Primo Levi.
15 *The Double Bond* by Carole Angier, p. 423.
16 'Buna' from *Collected Poems* by Primo Levi.
17 *The Truce* by Primo Levi.
18 'Lorenzo's Return' in *Moments of Reprieve* by Primo Levi.
19 'Lorenzo's Return' in *Moments of Reprieve* by Primo Levi.
20 *Primo Levi: A Life* by Ian Thomson.
21 *Ibid.*
22 *If Not Now, When?* by Primo Levi.
23 *Ibid.*
24 *Ibid.*
25 *Primo Levi: A Life* by Ian Thomson.
26 Michele Tavella to Carlo Greppi, 29 January 2020.
27 Manfredi, *Il Cielo sopra il Castello*, p. 127.
28 *Ibid*, p. 437.
29 *The Search for Roots* by Primo Levi.
30 'Potassium' in *The Periodic Table* by Primo Levi.
31 'Bear Meat' in *A Tranquil Star* by Primo Levi.
32 *The Wrench* by Primo Levi.
33 *Ibid.*
34 *Ibid.*
35 'Bear Meat' in *A Tranquil Star* by Primo Levi.
36 *The Truce* by Primo Levi.
37 'Arsenic' in *The Periodic Table* by Primo Levi.
38 *The Drowned and the Saved* by Primo Levi.
39 'Iron' in *The Periodic Table* by Primo Levi.
40 'Small Reed Lights' in *The Sixth Day* by Primo Levi.
41 The story is called 'The Squirrel', it appears in the collection *Other People's Trades* by Primo Levi (1985).

CHAPTER 11: FROM ONE WHO ALWAYS REMEMBERS YOU

1 'Lorenzo's Return' in *Moments of Reprieve* by Primo Levi.
2 *The Drowned and the Saved* by Primo Levi.
3 Michele Tavella to Carlo Greppi, 7 July 2022.
4 Giuseppe Perone to Carlo Greppi, 29 January 2020.
5 *The Search for Roots* by Primo Levi.
6 'The Molecule's Defiance' in *A Tranquil Star* by Primo Levi.
7 'Chromium' in *The Periodic Table* by Primo Levi.
8 *Ibid.*
9 *Ibid.*

10   *Ibid.*
11   *The Double Bond* by Carole Angier, p. 424.
12   *Ibid.*, p. 424–5.
13   *Other People's Trades* by Primo Levi.
14   *Primo Levi, l'amico* by Giudetti Serra, p. 12.
15   *If This Is A Man* by Primo Levi.
16   *The Drowned and the Saved* by Primo Levi.

CHAPTER 12: AND THEY WILL PAY BACK

1   'Lorenzo's Return' in *Moments of Reprieve* by Primo Levi.
2   *L'Importanza di Lorenzo Perone nelle opere di Primo Levi* by Samuele Saleri, pp. 75–6.
3   Giovanni Niffenegger to Carlo Greppi, 28 July 2022.
4   *Primo Levi: A Life* by Ian Thomson.
5   *Manuale di alcologia, Edizioni Centro Studi Erickson* by Vladimir Hudolin, (Trento, 2015) (I ed. 1991), p. 221.
6   *The Double Bond* by Carole Angier, p. 424.
7   *Ibid*, p. 423.
8   *Ibid*, p. 423.
9   *Ibid*, p. 423.
10 Ian Thomson to Carlo Greppi, 19 July 2022.
11 *Primo Levi: A Life* by Ian Thomson.
12 *Primo Levi: A Life* by Ian Thomson.
13 *The Drowned and the Saved* by Primo Levi.
14 *Primo Levi: A Life* by Ian Thomson.
15 *Il Cielo sopra il Castello* by Beppe Manfredi, p. 252.
16 *The Double Bond* by Carole Angier, p. 424.
17 *Primo Levi: A Life* by Ian Thomson.

CHAPTER 13: THE STORY OF A HOLY DRINKER

1   I am grateful to Ian Thomson for suggesting that I give a chapter of the book this title. The reference is to Joseph Roth's wonderful story *The Legend of the Holy Drinker*.
2   'Lorenzo's Return' in *Moments of Reprieve* by Primo Levi.
3   *The Drowned and the Saved* by Primo Levi.
4   *Ibid.*
5   *Ibid.*
6   'Lorenzo's Return' in *Moments of Reprieve* by Primo Levi.
7   *The Search for Roots* by Primo Levi.
8   *The Drowned and the Saved* by Primo Levi.
9   *Ibid.*

NOTES

10 *The Search for Roots* by Primo Levi.
11 'Renzo's Fist' in *Other People's Trades* by Primo Levi.
12 *The Drowned and the Saved* by Primo Levi.
13 *Ibid.*
14 *The Truce* by Primo Levi.
15 'Lorenzo's Return' in *Moments of Reprieve* by Primo Levi.

CHAPTER 14: THE LAST WORD

1 Claudio Mana to the author, 18 October 2022.
2 Silvio Pagliero to the author, 10 February 2020 and 28 June 2022.
3 Piotr Cywínski to the author, 18 September 2022.
4 Samuele Saleri to the author, 18 March 2022.
5 Jan Brokken to the author, 2 October 2022.
6 *Reading Primo Levi* by David Grossman in 'Robinson' supplement of *La Repubblica*, 5 November 2017.
7 Cesare Bermani to the author, 26 October 2022.
8 Ian Thomson to the author, 19 July 2022.
9 Luca Bedino to the author, 21 April 2022.
10 'Zinc' in *The Periodic Table* by Primo Levi.
11 *The Double Bond* by Carole Angier, p. 143.
12 *The Double Bond* by Carole Angier, p. 302.
13 Emma Barberis to the author, 9 September 2022.

SOURCES

ARCHIVES

Auschwitz Archives
Archivio Carole Angier at Centro Internazionale di Studi Primo Levi
Archivio di Stato di Cuneo
Archivio Primo Levi
Archivio Yad Vashem, file of LP
Arolsen Archives
Archivio storico dell'Archivio generale del Comune di Cuneo
Archivio storico della Città di Fossano
Archivio di Stato di Piacenza
Camera di Commercio di Cuneo
Camera di Commercio di Piacenza
Ian Thomson Collection at The Wiener Holocaust Library, London

WORKS FREQUENTLY CITED

Angier, Carole, *The Double Bond: Primo Levi, A Biography* (Farrar, Straus and Giroux, 2002)
Levi, Primo, *A Tranquil Star*, translated by Ann Goldstein and Alessandra Bastagli (Penguin, 2007)
Levi, Primo, *Collected Poems*, translated by Ruth Feldman and Brian (Swann, 1988)
Levi, Primo, *If Not Now, When?* translated by William Weaver (Simon and Schuster, 1985)
Levi, Primo, *If This Is A Man*, translated by Stuart Woolf (The Orion Press, 1959)
Levi, Primo, *Moments of Reprieve*, translated by Ruth Feldman (Summit Books, 1986)
Levi, Primo, *Other People's Trades*, translated by Raymond Rosenthal (Abacus, 1985)
Levi, Primo, *The Drowned and the Saved,* translated by Raymond Rosenthal (Michael Joseph, 1988)
Levi, Primo, *The Mirror Maker,* translated by Raymond Rosenthal (Abacus, 1986)
Levi, Primo, *The Periodic Table*, translated by Rosemary Rosenthal (Shocken Books, 1984)

SOURCES

Levi, Primo, *The Search for Roots*, translated by Peter Forbes (Allen Lane, 2001)

Levi, Primo, *The Sixth Day and Other Tales,* translated by Raymond Rosenthal (Summit Books, 1990)

Levi, Primo, *The Truce*, translated by Stuart Woolf (Abacus, 1965)

Levi, Primo, *The Voice of Memory*, translated by Robert Gordon (Polity, 2000)

Levi, Primo, *The Wrench,* translated by William Weaver (Michael Joeseph, 1987)

Thomson, Ian, *Primo Levi: A Life* (Henry Holt, 2014)

CREDITS

We are grateful to the copyright holders who have granted permission to use selected extracts and illustrations in this work.

PRIMO LEVI

If This Is A Man translated by Stuart Woolf, 1959 (Everyman, 2000)
'To my Friends', 'Mandate' and 'Burna' from *Collected Poems* translated by Ruth Feldman and Brian Swann (Faber & Faber, 1992)
'Lorenzo's Return' in *Moments of Reprieve* translated by Ruth Feldman (Penguin Modern Classics, 1986)
The Drowned and the Saved translated by Raymond Rosenthal (Abacus, 1988)
'Arsenic' and 'Chromium' from *The Periodic Table* translated by Raymond Rosenthal (Abacus, 1984)
If Not Now, When? translated by William Weaver (Penguin Classics, 1985)
The Wrench translated by William Weaver (Abacus, 1987)
The Search for Roots translated by Peter Forbes (Allen Lane, 2001)
The Truce translated by Stuart Wolf (Everyman, 1959)

IAN THOMSON
Primo Levi: A Life (Vintage, 2003)

CAROLE ANGIER
The Double Bond: Primo Levi, a Biography (Viking, 2002)

ILLUSTRATIONS
p. 6 Lorenzo Perrone, courtesy of Emma Barberis; p. 11 Fossano near the railway station, photograph of the Corrado Ponzo collection in Guido and Sandro Alessandrini; p. 12 Borgo Vecchio di Fossano, Michele Tavella's private archive, historical photos of the Borgo Vecchio; p. 18 Lorenzo Perrone during his military service, the Primo Levi Collection, The Wiener Holocaust Library, London; p. 39 the note that Primo Levi wrote to Bianca Guidetti Serra while traveling to Auschwitz, the Primo Levi Archive; p. 53 the distribution of soup in Monowitz, The Archive of the State Museum Auschwitz-Birkenau in Oświęcim; p. 74 Lorenzo Perrone's canteen

card, Antonio Martorello's private archive; p. 87 the first letter sent by Lorenzo Perrone from Primo Levi, the Primo Levi Archive; p. 105 the third letter sent by Lorenzo Perrone to Primo Levi from Auschwitz, the Primo Levi Archive; p. 120 Lorenzo Perrone's passport, Carole Angier's archive; p. 156 apprentice bricklayers, Michele Tavella's private archive, photo historical buildings of the Borgo Vecchio; p. 157 Young Fossanese villagers with the curate Don Cavallo, Michele Tavella's private archive, historical photos of the Borgo Vecchio; p. 158 postcard sent by Lorenzo Perrone to Primo Levi, the Primo Levi archive; p. 197 Primo Levi with his son Renzo, the Primo Levi Archive; p. 204 Casa Perrone, the Claudio Archive Mana.

INDEX

Aigues-Mortes massacre (1893) 26
Aleichem, Shalom 190
Améry, Jean (Hans Chaim Mayer) 189
Angier, Carole 113–4, 128–9, 142–3
   archives 120, 145, 159, 198
   book research 209
   celebrating Lorenzo xii, 132
   Lenta and 177
   Lorenzo as a 'Righteous Among the Nations' 213
   'Lorenzo is crucial' 206, 208
   observations 84, 111, 144
   Perrone family and 127, 134, 137, 175–6, 181
   reconstructing events 29, 122, 173
   supporters of Levi biography 200
Antonio Dutto & Sons 168–70
Antonio (prisoner) 98
Arolsen Archives 33, 74, 85, 97
Artom, Emanuele 37
Auschwitz 3, 58
   See also Birkenau; Monowitz-Buna
Auschwitz-Birkenau Memorial and Museum 32, 47, 74, 204, 205
Ausweis (foreign worker ID) 32–3
Axis Alliance 30–1

Barberis, Emma (niece) 55, 65, 128–9, 134, 145, 155, 157, 175, 176, 180, 181, 196, 209
Basik, Wojciech 47
Bedino, Luca 207
Beotti 31, 33, 51, 52, 64, 85, 98, 114, 154–5
Bermani, Cesare 23, 28, 29, 74, 206
Bertotti, Don 148
Bertotti, Francesco 148

Bertrand, Louis, *L'Invasion* 26
Bielski brothers 48
Birkenau concentration camp 47, 68 76, 84, 115–6, 204
Blechhammer 92–3
Bocca, Giorgio 152, 201
Borgo Vecchio, Fossano 12, 142, 156, 177, 203
Boschwitz, Ulrich Alexander 60
Brecht, Bertolt 214
Brokken, Jan 206
Browning, Christopher R. 83
Bruck-an-der-Mur, Austria 114–5
Bucciantini, Massimo 51
Buchenwald concentration camp 117
Buna/Monowitz *see* Monowitz-Buna concentration camp
Burgué, Fossano 10–1, *11*, 20–1, 29, 59, 131, 143, 147–8, 156–7, *156*, 180, 203, 204
Busicchia, Giovanni 50

Cademartiri, Pietro 74
Camp Leonhard Haag, Lager 32, 112
Caracciolo, Nicola 76, 141, 152, 161, 171
Carbide Tower, Buna 64–5
Cavaglion, Alberto xii
Cavallo, Don 157
Chiappano, Alessandra 36
Colombo 98, 111, 113–4, 155
Conreau, Charles 135
Corbin, Alain 214
Corriere Subalpino 21–2
Cosa, Piero 14
Côte d'Azur 9–10, 26
Courage and the Pity, The ix
Coward, Charles 93
Cuneo 25–7, 129, 168–9

INDEX

Cywiński, Piotr 47–8, 205–6

Dachau concentration camp 98
Daimler 51
Dalla Volta, Alberto 41, 53, 63, 66, 75, 77, 79, 83, 91–2, 93, 95, 102, 104, 106, 108, 115, 116–7, 129, 136
Dalla Volta, Emma 143, 159
Dalla Volta, Guido 41
De Benedetti, Leonardo 167
Della Torre, Ada 37, 88
Delmastro, Sandro 99–100, 102, 151
Demichelis, Alessandra 20–1
Deutsche Erd- und Steinwerke GmbH 52
Dronero 19
Ducarne, Arthur 135
Dutto, Aldo 168, 169
Dutto, Antonio 168–70
Dutto, Caterina 169
Dutto, Oreste 169

Einaudi 65, 164–5, 196
Elias (prisoner) 102
escapees 47, 75, 92–4, 96, 112
Ettore (prisoner) 98
extermination camps 47, 76, 84, 104, 115–6, 132, 204

Famiglia Cristiana 201
Fascism, rise and fall of 18–20, 25, 28, 35–6, 52, 59
Fenoglio, Beppe 203
Fontana, Laura *Gli italiani ad Auschwitz* 75, 85
Fossano 9–13, 11–2, 129–31, 136–7, 147–8, 155–7, 156–7, 169–70, 177
  Bastione del Salice 29
  celebration of Lorenzo 207, 211–2
  community spirit 92
  development of 17–8, 25
  Fascism in 19, 74
  population 123, 142, 152, 179
  post-war 129–30

Viale delle Alpi plaque 212–3
  view of *158*, 159
Fossoli concentration camp 36, 117
France 25–7, 28–31

G. Beotti *see* Beotti
gas chambers 3, 40–1, 46, 76, 115, 116
Genoa uprising (1945) 20
Genola 123, 127–8
Gentili Tedeschi, Eugenio 37
Germanetto, Giovanni 19
Gotfryd, Jean 34
Gross, Jan Tomasz 94
Grossman, David 206
Guidetti Serra, Bianca 36, 39, *39*, 88, 90–1, 117–8, 135, 161, 200–1
  Bianca la rossa 86

Heydebreck 93
Holocaust ix–xi
Horwitz, Gordon J. 52

I. G. Farben 3, 7, 51, 52, 74, 84, 109–10, 116
Il Popolo Fossanese 178, 201, 211
Italian Social Republic 35–6

Jona, Lino 37
Judge of the Righteous, The x

Kamlah, Wilhelm 190

La Fedeltà 129–30, 131, 133, 169, 177
Lenta, Don Carlo 16, 92, 142, 176–8, 179–80, 181, 207, 211
Levaldigi 31, 155
Levi, Anna Maria 56, 90, 104, 122–3, 135, 136
Levi, Cesare 134–5, 152
Levi family 15, 88–91, 152, 167
Levi, Lisa Lorenza x, 166–7, 181, 183, 210
Levi, Primo
  before Auschwitz 36, 38
  correspondence with Lorenzo

158–9, *158*, 159, 162, 163, 166–7, 206
correspondence with friends, family 104–5, *105*, 88–9, 90, 91, 197, 117–8
on food 50, 53, 75–6, 83
on hope 119
on Jewish prisoners 7
on Lorenzo ix, x–xi, 3–8, 25, 40, 58–9, 100–1, 109, 117–9, 141–2, 144, 193–4, 181, 183, 187–8, 197
on writing 135, 160
marriage and children 160, 166–7
military papers 138
on the Piedmontese dialect 150–1
scarlet fever 108, 109, 116, 117
suicide 187–90
visits 136–7, 152–3, 175, 196
works in the polymerisation laboratory 107–8
'A Disciple' 86
Auschwitz, città tranquilla 98–9
Buna 138–40
'Cesare's Last Adventure' 101
The Complete Works of Primo Levi 198, 200
The Drowned and the Saved ix–x, 3, 41, 51, 60, 78–80, 91–2, 188–9, 191, 198, 199
'Guests' 150
If Not Now, When? 40, 48, 55–6, 71, 84, 146–7
If This Is A Man ix, x–xi, 37–8, 40–1, 43, 45, 49, 57, 64, 77–8, 80, 84, 103, 106, 118–9, 134, 135, 140, 161, 163–5, 196–8, 202, 211
If This Is A Man (play) 65–9, 73, 76, 81–2, 198, 199
'Iron' 99
'The Guerrino Valley' 143
'The Juggler' 88
'The Squirrel' 201
'Last Christmas of the War' 104, 201
'Lorenzo's Return', 79–80, 97, 102, 112, 122, 142, 159, 170, 187, 193, 198, 202, 211
Mandate 215
Moments of Reprieve ix, 31, 55, 80–1, 84, 86, 95, 101–2, 106–7, 140–1, 177, 190, 211
Natural Histories 185
Other People's Trades 99, 192, 201
The Periodic Table 6, 99–100, 136, 198
'Potassium' 100
'Renzo's Fist' 192
The Search for Roots 148–9, 159, 191–2
The Sixth Day and Other Tales 125
Storie naturali 34–5
A tempo debito 174–5
'The Molecule's Defiance' 159
'To My Friends' 1
The Truce 23–5, 45, 102, 111, 136, 138, 150, 192–3, 196, 201
'Versamina' 185
'Westward' 125
The Wrench 30, 35, 41, 56, 145–6, 149–50
Levi, Renzo x, 196, *197*, 201, 210, 212
Lusa, Pietro and Giuseppina 85–6
Luzzati, Ester 'Rina' 88–9, 90, 91, 104, 122, 135
Luzzati family 134

Macho, Thomas 189
Maestro, Vanda 36, 37, 39, 117
Malaquais, Jean 26
Mana, Claudio 203
Manfredi, Mayor Giuseppe 132, 148, 172–3, *176*, 181, 202, 203, 209, 211–2
Mantelli, Brunello 74
Marché, Pieralberto (Pieralberto Marchesini) 65–9, 73, 76, 81–2
Marengo, Francesco 179
Martorello, Antonio 147, 206
Mauthausen concentration camp 117
Mellano, Luisa 14, 212

INDEX

Menardi, Giovanni 156, 213
migration 25–7
Mioni, Bruno 85
Mioni, Umberto 85
Modiano, Patrick, *Dora Bruder* 214
Momigliano, Franco 37
Mondovì 18
Monowitz-Buna concentration camp 3–5, 7–8, 32, 34, 47, 53, *53*, 74–5, *74*, 84, 93, 94, 107, 115–6, 204
Morpurgo, Lucia 160, 166–7, 181, 183
Morra, Carlo 172, 174
Motola, Gabriel 143, 170, 187

National Liberation Committee 122–3, 130–1
Nezri-Dufour, Sophie 138
Niffenegger, Dr Giovanni 172, 175–6
Nissim, Luciana 36, 37, 39
Nuremberg trials (1945–46) 52

Ortona, Silvio 37

Pagani 85–6
Pagliero, Silvio 203
Paldiel, Mordecai x, 132
Perlasca, Giorgio xi
Perone family 9, 13–16, 121–2, 128–9, 132, 133, 157, 173, 176, 182, 200, 202, *204*, 212
Perrone, Beppe (nephew) 10, 13, 55, 157, 209
Perrone, Caterina 'Nina' (sister) 13, 157, 161, 175, 182, 203, 209
Perrone, Giovanna (sister) 13, 54, 65, 128, 157, 175, 182, 197
Perrone, Giovanni (brother) 9–10, 14, 130–1, 157, 161, 182
Perrone, Giuseppe (father) 13, 15, 33, 128, 132, 182
Perrone, Lorenzo 14–6, 49–50, 75–7
  alcoholic 141–2, 144, 149–50, 171, 173, 174–5, 187–8, 189
  Camp Leonhard 32, 110, 111–14
  correspondence 105–6, 159, 162, 163, 166–7, 206
  death 132–3, 178–83, 187–8
  employment 9–10, 27, 28, 29, 29–30, 31–2, 33
  family and background 8–16
  Fascism and 19–20
  feramiù (junk dealer) 14, 142
  food stamps 74
  health 110, 170–2, 187
  knitted vest from Levi 137–8
  letters by *87*, *105*
  Levi on ix, x–xi, 25, 100–1, 109, 117–9, 141–2, 144
  mess tin 41, 50, 64, 77, 95, 102, 109–10, 128–9, 151
  military 17, *18*, 27
  note to Bianca Guidetti Serra 39
  passport 41, 120–1, *120*, 138
  photographs of 6, *18*, 121, 161, 202
  postcard sent to Levi 158–9, *158*
  postcards sent by 33, 85, 86–7, 88, 90, 105–6
  relationship with Levi 3–8, 40, 58–9, 121–2
  'saintliness' 193–4, 208
Perrone, Michele (brother) 10, 13, 132–3, 157, 175–6, 178, 182
Perrone, Secondo (brother) 13, 132, 144–5, 175–6
Peruch (prisoner) 96–8, 110, 112, 114, 115, 121, 129
Perugia, Lello 102
Piacenza 64, 85, 154
Piacenza, Aldo 36
Piedmontese immigrants 26–7
'Pigher', Fossano pub 13–4, 20, 133, 147–8, 151, 204, 209
Pinagot, Louis-François 214
Primo Levi Archive 33, 85
Primo Levi International Study Centre 57, 113, 159

Revelli, Nuto 21
Ricciotti, Lazzero 121
'Righteous Among the Nations' x,

47, 94, 132, 177, 202, 210, 211–3
Romita, Domenico 211
Rosenfeld, Prof Alvin 109, 113, 122, 142, 171, 194, 198
Rosi, Francesco, *The Truce* 199, 209
Roth, Philip 108

Sacerdoti, Franco 37, 108
Saleri, Samuele 137–8, 156, 206, 212, 213
Salmoni, Alberto 36
Samuel, Jean 136, 201
Santa Caterina 19–20
Saporiti 155
Sauckel, Fritz 73
Scappini, Remo 20
Scarpa, Domenico 200
Scheingesicht, Mendel 94
Schindler, Oskar xi, 178
Schindler's List xi, 178
Scholten, Yvonne 213
Segre, Giorgio 37
Setkiewicz, Piotr 50, 75, 116
shoes, importance of 45–6, 54, 62–4, 106–7
Siemens 51
SIVA (Società Industriale Vernici e Affini) 166
Sobibor extermination camp 47
Sordo, Cino 123, 127–8
Spinetta, Cuneo 168–9
Stajano, Corrado 193
Starachowice concentration camp 83
Staryje Doroghi 111
Stawinoga (laboratory manager) 107
Suetta, Angelo 19
suicide 104, 187–90
Szántó, Endre 'Bandi' 89–90, 102

Tacca (troublemakers) 12–15, 20–3, 40
Tallone, Giovanna (mother) 13, 128–9, 145, 161, 209
Tavella, Michele 143, 147, 157–8
Tec, Nechama 48
Thomson, Ian 144–5, 198–9, 206–7

book research 84, 123, 209
Lenta and 16, 92, 177, 207
on letters 88
Lorenzo's death 180
Perrone family and 132, 134, 142, 147
reconstructing events 91, 122, 173
Thyssen-Krupp 51
Treblinka extermination camp 47
Trimmer, Jacob Max 94
tuberculosis 37, 170–4, 187–9

Upper Silesia 3, 28, 31

Valle, Giuseppe 203
Vanzetti, Bartolomeo 14
Vermicelli, Gino 23
Via Michelini, Fossano 10, 123, 127–8, 131, 147, 180, 203–4, *204*
Vincenti, Fiora 201
Vincenti, Guillermo 212
'volunteer' workers 73–5

Warsaw Ghetto Uprising (1943) 47
Wiener Holocaust Library, London 173
Wolf, Robert 47
Wrona family 94
Wrona, Józef 94

Yad Vashem x, xii, 15, 31, 94, 113, 144, 179, 198, 200, 212–3

Zakłady Chemiczne 204
Zwick, Edward 48